مَبَادِئُ الإِسْلاَمْ
Basics of Islam

Abdul Hye, PhD

Where Do You Stand?
Houston, Texas

Basics of Islam

Published by:
Where Do You Stand?
P.O. Box - 890071
Houston, Texas 77289
www.WhereDoYouStand.net
www.islamicbooks4u.com
a6h@yahoo.com
281-488-3191

1st print: July / 1999
2nd print: October / 2006

Printed in the United States of America

Library of Congress Catalog Card Number: 98-94027

ISBN 0-9668190-0-4

Table of Contents

Introduction

With the help of Allah ﷻ, this book is revised for young, adult Muslims, and new Muslims to provide basic Islamic knowledge, and to use in everyday life. All explanations are in direct form. Many items are formatted in the form of flow diagrams. All Arabic writings are followed by English pronunciation *in Italics* and English meaning (in parentheses). This should help those who can not read Arabic and new Muslims to understand and use them properly.

Abdul Hye, PhD
Houston, Texas
October / 2006

Chapter – 1: Iman and Tauhid

Iman / Belief: To a Muslim, Iman means firm belief in Allah ﷻ and the teachings of Rasul ﷺ.

There are 5 kalimas / sayings which define Iman / Belief:

1st Kalima (Tayaba - Oneness of Allah)

لَاإِلٰهَ اَلَّااللهُ مُحَمَّدٌ رَّسُوْلُ اللهِ

La ilaha illallahu Muhammadur Rasulullah ﷺ (There is none worthy of worship but Allah. Muhammad (*sallallaho alaihe wasallam*) is Allah's Messenger).

2nd Kalima (Sahadat - Testification of Allah)

اَشْهَدُ اَنْ لَّاإِلٰهَ اِلَّا اللهُ وَاَشْهَدُ اَنَّ مُحَمَّدًا عَبْدُه وَرَسُوْلُه

Ash-hadu allah ilaha ilallahu wash-hadu anna Muhammadun abduhu warasuluhu. (I testify that there is none worthy of worship but Allah and I testify that Muhammad (*sallallahu alaihe wasallam*) is Allah's worshipper and Messenger).

3rd Kalima (Tamjeed - Glorification of Allah)

سُبْحَانَ اللهِ وَالْحَمْدُ لِلهِ وَلَا اِلٰهَ اِلَّا اللهُ وَاللهُ اَكْبَرُ وَلَاحَوْلَ وَلَا قُوَّةَ اِلَّا بِاللهِ الْعَلِى الْعَظِيْمِ

Subhan allahe walhamdulillah wala ilaha illallahu wallahu akbar wala haula wala quwwata illa billahel aliul azim. (Glory is to Allah. All praise is to Allah. There is none worthy of worship besides Allah. And Allah is the greatest. There is no power and might except from Allah. The most high - The great).

4th Kalima (Tauhid - Unity of Allah)

لَا اِلٰهَ اِلَّا اللهُ وَحْدَهُ لَاشَرِيْكَ لَهُ لَهُ الْمُلْكُ وَلَهُ الْحَمْدُ يُحْيِىْ وَيُمِيْتُ بِيَدِهِ الْخَيْرُ وَهُوَ عَلٰى كُلّ شَىءٍ قَدِيْرٌ

La ilaha illallahu wahdahu lasharika lahu lahul mulku walahul hamdu ehue wayamitu biyadihil khairu wahua ala kulle shaiyyen qadir. (There is none worthy of worship besides Allah, Who is alone, He has no partner, His is the kingdom and for Him is all praise. He gives life and causes death. In His hand is all good and He has power over everything).

5th Kalima (Radde Kufr - Disapproval of Kufr)

اَللّٰهُمَّ اِنِّىْ اَعُوْذُبِكَ مِنْ اَنْ اُشْرِكَ بِكَ شَيْئًا وَّاَنَا اَعْلَمُ بِهِ وَاَسْتَغْفِرُكَ لِمَا لَاۤ اَعْلَمُ بِهِ
تُبْتُ عِنْهُ وَتَبَرَّاتُ مِنَ الْكُفْرِ وَالشِّرْكِ وَالْكِذْبِ ـ وَالْمَعَاصِىْ كُلِّهَا اَسْلَمْتُ وَاٰمَنْتُ
وَاَقُوْلُ لَاۤ اِلٰهَ اِلَّا اللّٰهُ مُحَمَّدٌ رَّسُوْلُ اللّٰهِ

Allahumma inni auzubeka min un ushreka bika shaiau wa ana aalamu bihi wa astagh feruka lemala aalamu bihi tubtu anhu wata barratu minul kufre wash sherke wal kezbe wal maasi kulleha aslumtu wamuntu waqulu la ilaha illallahu muhammadur Rasulullah ﷺ. (O Allah! I seek protection in You from that I should join any partner with You knowingly. I seek Your forgiveness from that which I do not know. I repent from it (ignorance). I free myself from disbelief and joining partners with You and from all sins. I submit to Your will I believe and I declare: There is none worthy of worship besides Allah and Muhammad (sallallahu alaihe wasallam) is Allah's Messenger).

Basis of Iman

Imane Mujmal

اٰمَنْتُ بِاللهِ كَمَا هُوَ بِاَسْمَائِهِ وَصِفَاتِهِ وَقَبِلْتُ جَمِيْعَ اَحْكَامِهِ

Amantu billahe kamahua beasmaihi wasifatihi wakabeltu jamia ahkamihi. (I believe in Allah as He is with His many names and qualities and I have accepted all His orders).

Imane Mufassal

اٰمَنْتُ بِاللهِ وَمَلَئِكَتِهِ وَكُتُبِهِ وَرُسُلِهِ وَالْيَوْمِ الْاٰخِرِ وَالْقَدْرِ خَيْرِهِ وَشَرِّهِ مِنَ اللهِ تَعَالٰى وَالْبَعْثِ بَعْدَ الْمَوْتِ

Amantu billahe wama laikatihi wakutubihi warasulihi wal yaomel akhiri wal qadre khairihi washarrihi minallahe taala walbase badal mout. (I believe in Allah, His Angeles, His Books, His Messengers, in the Day of Judgment, Fate-good and bad is from Allah and life after death).

Who is Allah?

1. Allah is one and has no partners.
2. He is the only one worthy of worship and none besides Allah is worthy of worship.
3. He knows thoughts that go into a person's mind, nothing is hidden from Him.
4. He is most powerful.
5. He has created earth, skies, sun, moon, stars, and angels, human and whole universe.
6. He gives life and death.
7. He gives sustenance to all creation.
8. He does not eat, drink or sleep.
9. He is forever and will be forever.
10. He was not created by anyone.
11. He does not have parents, wife or children.
12. He does not depend on anybody, all depends on Him.
13. Nobody resembles Him, He resembles none.
14. He is pure from all faults.
15. He does not have eyes, nose or body like human.
16. Allah has 99 names (attributes) -

99 Names of Allah ﷻ

1: *Allah* (The Name of Allah) اَللهُ
2: *Ar-Rahman* (The Compassionate) اَلرَّحْمنُ
3: *Ar-Rahim* (The Merciful) اَلرَّحِيْمُ
4: *Al-Malik* (The King). اَلْمَلِكُ
5: *Al-Quddus* (The Holy) اَلْقُدُّوْسُ
6: *As-Salam* (The Source of Peace) اَلسَّلَامُ
7: *Al-Mumin* (The Guardian of Faith) اَلْمُؤْمِنُ
8: *Al-Muhymin* (The Guardian) اَلْمُهَيْمِنُ
9: *Al-Aziz* (The Mighty) اَلْعَزِيْزُ
10: *Al-Jabbar)* (The Enforcer) اَلْجَبَّارُ
11: *Al-Mutakabbir* (The Supreme) اَلْمُتَكَبِّرُ
12: *Al-Khaliq* (The Creator) اَلْخَالِقُ
13: *Al-Bari* (The Evolver) اَلْبَارِئُ
14: *Al-Musawwir* (The Fashioner) اَلْمُصَوِّرُ

15: *Al-Gaffar* (The Forgiver) اَلْغَقَّارُ

16: *Al-Qahhar* (The Subduer) اَلْقَهَّارُ

17: *Al-Wahhab* (The Bestower) اَلْوَهَّابُ

18: *Ar-Razzaq* (The Provider) اَلرَّزَّاقُ

19: *Al-Fattah* (The Opener) اَلْفَتَّاحُ

20: *Al-Alim* (The All Knowing) اَلْعَلِيْمُ

21: *Al-Qabid* (The Seizer) اَلْقَابِضُ

22: *Al-Basit*(The Expander) اَلْبَاسِطُ

23: *Al-Khafid* (The Abaser) اَلْخَافِضُ

24: *Ar-Rafi* (The Exalter) اَلرَّافِعُ

25: *Al-Muizz* (The Dignifier) اَلْمُعِزُّ

26: *Al-Mujill* (The Humiliator) اَلْمُذِلّ

27: *As-Sami* (The All-Hearing) اَلسَّمِيْعُ

28: *Al-Basir* (The All-Seeing) اَلْبَصِيْرُ

29: *Al-Hakam* (The Judge) اَلْحَكَمُ

30: *Al-Adl* (The just) اَلْعَدْلُ

31: *Al-Latif* (The Subtle) اَللَّطِيْفُ

32: *Al-Khabir* (The Aware) اَلْخَبِيْرُ

33: *Al-Halim* (The Forbearing) اَلْحَلِيْمُ

34: *Al-Azim* (The Magnificent) اَلْعَظِيْمُ

35: *Al-Gafur* (The Forgiver) اَلْغَفُوْرُ

36: *Ash-Sakur* (The Appreciative) اَلشَّكُوْرُ

37: *Al-Ali* (The Most High) اَلْعَلِىُّ

38: *Al-Kabir* (The Most Great) اَلْكَبِيْرُ

39: *Al-Hafiz* (The Preserver) اَلْحَفِيْظُ

40: *Al-Muqit* (The Nourisher) اَلْمُقِيْتُ

41: *Al-Hasib* (The Reckoner) اَلْحَسِيْبُ

42: *Al-Jalil* (The Glorious) اَلْجَلِيْلُ

43: *Al-Karim* (The Munificent) اَلْكَرِيْمُ

44: *Al-Raqib* (The Vigilant) اَلرَّقِيْبُ

45: *Al-Mujib* (The Responder to Prayer) اَلْمُجِيْبُ

46: *Al-Wasi* (The All-Embracing) اَلْةاسِعُ

47: *Al-Hakim* (The Wise) اَلْحَكِيْمُ

48: *Al-Wadud* (The Loving) اَلْوَدُوْدُ

49: *Al-Majid* (The Majestic) اَلْمَجِيْدُ
50: *Al-Baith* (The Resurrector) اَلْبَاعِثُ
51: *As-Sahid* (The Witness) اَلشَّهِيْدُ
52: *Al-Haq* (The Truth) اَلْحَقُّ
53: *Al-Wakil* (The Ultimate Trustee) اَلْوَكِيْلُ
54: *Al-Qawi* (The Strong) اَلْقَوِىُّ
55: *Al-Matin* (The Firm) اَلْمَتِيْنُ
56: *Al-Wali* (The Protector) اَلْوَلِىُّ
57: *Al-Hamid* (The Praiseworthy) اَلْحَمِيْدُ
58: *Al-Mushi* (The Appraiser) اَلْمُحْصِىْ
59: *Al-Mubdi* (The Originator) اَلْمُبْدِىُ
60: *Al-Muid* (The Restorer) اَلْمُعِيْدُ
61: *Al-Muhyi* (The Giver of Life) اَلْمُحْىِىْ
62: *Al-Mumit* (The Giver of Death) اَلْمُمِيْتُ
63: *Al-Hye* (The Eternal) اَلْحَىُّ
64: *Al-Qayyum* (The Self Existing) اَلْقَيُّوْمُ
65: *Al-Wajid* (The Finder) اَلْوَاجِدُ
66: *Al-Majid* (The Splendid) اَلْمَاجِدُ
67: *Al-Wahid* (The One) اَلْوَاحِدُ *Al-Ahad* (The Unique) اَلْاَحَدُ
68: *As-Samad* (The Absolute) اَلصَّمَدُ
69: *Al-Qadir* (The Able) لْقَادِرُ
70: *Al-Muqtadir* (The Powerful) اَلْمُقْتَدِرُ
71: *Al-Muqaddam* (The Expeditor) اَلْمُقَدِّمُ
72: *Al-Muakhhir* (The Delayer) اَلْمُؤَخِّرُ
73: *Al-Awal* (The First) اَلْاَوَّلُ
74: *Al-Akir* (The Last) اَلْاخِرُ
75: *Az-Zahir* (The Manifest) اَلظَّاهِرُ
76: *Al-Batin* (The Hidden) اَلْبَاطِنُ
77: *Al-Wali* (The Supreme Governor) اَلْوَالِىْ
78: *Al-Mutaali* (The Most Exalted) اَلْمُتَعَالِىْ
79: *Al-Barr* (The Source of All Good) اَلْبَرُّ
80: *At-Tawwab* (The acceptor of Repentance) اَلتَّوَّابُ
81: *Al-Muntaqim* (The Avenger) اَلْمُنْتَقِمُ
82: *Al-Afu* (The Pardoner) اَلْعَفُوُّ

83: *Ar-Rauf* (The Clement) الرَّءُوْفُ
84: *Malik-ul-Mulk* (The Master of Sovereignty) مَالِكُ الْمُلْكِ
85: *Jul-Jalali-Wal-Ikram* (Lord of Majesty and Generosity)
ذُوالْجَلَالِ وَالاِكْرَام
86: *Al-Muqsit* (The Equitable) الْمُقْسِطُ
87: *Al-Jame* (The Gatherer) الْجَامِعُ
88: *Al-Gani* (The Self-Sufficient) الْغَنِىُّ
89: *Al-Mugni* (The Enricher) الْمُغْنِى
90: *Al-Mani* (The Preventor) الْمَانِعُ
91: *Ad-Dar* (The One who causes Loss) الضَّارُّ
92: *An-Nafi* (The Propitious) النَّافِعُ
93: *An-Nur* (The Light) النُّوْرُ
94: *Al-Hadi* (The Guide) لْهَادِى
95: *Al-Badi* (The Originator) الْبَدِيْعُ
96: *Al-Baqi* (The Everlasting) الْبَاقِىْ
97: *Al-Warith* (The Inheritor) الْوَارِثُ
98: *Al-Rashid* (The Righteous) الرَّشِيْدُ
99: *As-Sabur* (The Patient) الصَّبُوْرُ

What are the Angels?
1. Allah created them out of light and assigned different duties.
2. They are not visible to human.
3. They can not commit any sins nor disobey Allah.

4 Famous Angels
1. **Jibrael** – Responsible to bring Allah's books, orders and messages to all prophets, sent to help prophets at times and fight against their enemies.
2. **Michael** – Responsible for food and rain. Receives order from Allah. Other angels work under him on clouds, seas, rivers, and wind.
3. **Azrael** – Responsible to take away life to die at Allah's order. Other angels work under him – some take lives of good person, while others with fearful appearance take life of sinners and disbelievers.
4. **Israfel** – Responsible to blow trumpet to destroy universe on the day of judgment when Allah orders. Sound will destroy and kill everything on earth and in skies. All will come to life during second time blow with the order of Allah.

Other Important Angels

Kiraman-Katebin - Each person carries these 2 angels, Kiraman writes good and Katebin writes bad deeds.

Munkar and Nakir – These 2 angels are responsible to question a person after death in the grave.

Some angels are in charge of Heaven, some for Hell, some to look after children, old, weak and whom Allah wishes to protect. Qur'an and Hadith describe various angels who are in charge of various duties.

Books of Allah

1. Allah has revealed His Books to different Prophets for guidance to their nations. Big books are called Kitabs, small ones are called Sahifas.
2. **Four main revealed books**
   - **Torah** - (Old Testament) Prophet Musa *alaihe wasallam.*
   - **Zabor** - Prophet Dawood *alaihe wasallam.*
   - **Injel** - (New Testament) Prophet Isa *alaihe wasallam.*
   - **Qur'an** - Prophet Muhammed *sallallahu alaihe wasallam.*
3. 10 Sahifas – Prophet Adam, 50 Sahifas – Prophet Shees, 30 Sahifas – Prophet Idris, 10-30 Sahifas – Prophet Ibrahim. All books except Qur'an were revealed at once.
4. Qur'an was revealed over a period of 23 years.
5. No all books are in their original form – changes, alterations, and / or additions have been made. Qur'an is still in original form. No changes or alterations were made. It is memorized by heart by so many Hafez around the world at all times – from the beginning of Islam to present day. Allah has promised to safeguard the Qur'an and it is a miracle.

Messengers of Allah

1. Allah has sent many messengers to this world at different times to different areas to guide mankind.
2. These messengers are known as Rasuls and Nabis. The first messenger was Prophet Adam *alaihe wasallam*, last was Prophet Muhammad 襟.
3. There were about 124,000 Nabis. No person became a Nabi or Rasul by his own effort. All were pre-selected by Allah; they always spoke truth, committed no sins and conveyed the message

without adding or dropping anything. They all preached oneness of Allah. They performed miracles with the help of Allah.

4. All Rasuls were Nabis but not all Nabis were Rasuls. Rasul is a prophet who received new shariat / divine law and book from Allah. A Nabi follows the shariat of a Rasul before him. No prophet will come after our Nabi Muhammad ﷺ. He is the final prophet of Allah. Allah says in Qur'an as **Khatamun Nabiyen**, which means that he is the **last** of all Nabis.

5. Muhammad ﷺ is at the highest position amongst all the prophets.

6. There are 25 names of Nabis and Rasuls mentioned in the Qur'an:

Adam,	**Idris,**	**Nuh,**	**Hud,**	**Salih,**	**Ibrahim,**
Ishmail,	**Ishaq,**	**Lut,**	**Yakob,**	**Yusuf,**	**Shuaib,**
Ayub,	**Musa,**	**Harun,**	**Dhil-Kifl,**	**Dawood,**	**Suleman,**
Illyus,	**Al-Yasa,**	**Yunus,**	**Zakariyya,**	**Yahya,**	**'Isa,**
Muhammad.					

Sahaba / Companions of Muhammad ﷺ.

1. Any person (he or she) who saw Nabi Muhammad ﷺ even for a short time, embraced Islam and died as Muslim is called *Sahaba* ﷺ, *radiallahu anhu*. Rasul ﷺ said: All Sahaba *radiallahu anhum* are just and pious, whomsoever amongst them you shall follow, you will be guided. The highest rank amongst Sahaba is Abu Bakr till the day of Qiyamat. Next rank is Omar bin Khattab, then Osman, then Ali. Allah best knows positions of others.

2. 10 Sahaba received glad tidings of Paradise from Muhammad ﷺ in this world and they are called **Asharae Mubassara**. They are:

1. Abu Bakr,	**2. Omar,**	**3. Osman,**	**4. Ali,**	**5. Talha,**
6. Zubair,	**7. Abdur Rahman bin Auf,**			
8. Saad bin Abi Waqqas,	**9. Saed bin Zaid,**			
10. Abu Ubaidah bin Jarrah.				

3. It is from the Sahaba, people learnt Islam, Shariat / Islamic law was established, Sunnah of Muhammad ﷺ was obtained.

4. A non-Sahaba is not equal to the lowest Sahabi.

5. It is obligatory to show respect to all Sahaba and abstain from speaking ill and criticism.

Prophets mentioned in the Qur'an

(Links between prophets may or may not indicate direct descendants)

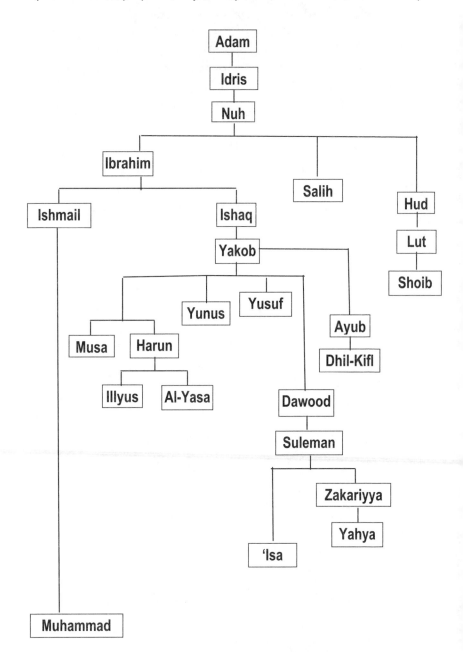

Fate / Taqdir

1. Allah knows everything before its creation.
2. Allah has given human beings willpower and ability to do good or bad.
3. Taqdir / Fate means belief in Allah's knowledge of good or bad things that would happen even before one is created.
4. All favors are from Allah only and no misfortune can happen except by the will of Allah.
5. One should not despair over any misfortune or boast over any favor. All comes from Allah. We should be thankful for His favors and be patient over any misfortune.

Last Day / Qiyamat

1. One day the world will come to an end. Only Allah knows when that day will be. Only this much is known that on one Friday, the 10th of Muharram, Angel Israfel will be ordered to blow the bugle. The sound from the bugle will cause every living creation to die.
2. The earth will be shaken, mountains will be like flakes of cotton wool, the sun and moon will crush, stars will lose their light and the whole universe will be destroyed.
3. Nabi Muhammad ﷺ mentioned the signs of approach of Qiyamat: People will…Disobey and disrespect their parents, break trust, singing, music and dancing will be common, Illiterate people will become leaders, speak ill of their ancestors and previous pious people, people with low income will begin to boast of high buildings, unworthy people will be given high posts.

Life after Death

1. After the day of Qiyamat when everything will be destroyed, angel Israfel will be ordered to blow the bugle for the second time.
2. Once again every person from Prophet Adam *alaihe wasallam* to the final day will be given new life. They will gather before Allah for judgment in the Field of Resurrection to give account of their deeds. The day is called Yaumul Hashar / Yaumud Deen / Yaumul Hisab.
3. People with good deeds will be rewarded with paradise / jannat. People with bad deeds will be punished in Hell / Jahannam. Besides kuffar / disbeliever and mushriken / makes partner with Allah, Allah will forgive whomever He wishes.

Chapter – 2: Istinja + Wudu + Gusl +Tayamum and Masah

Istinja means to clean private parts by tissue paper, clean water, and earth after passing urine and / or stool.

Two Types of Najasat / Filth

1. **Haqeqi** – Filth can be seen such as:
   - **Galiza** / heavy type - urine, stool of human, blood flow, wine.
   - **Kafifa** / light type- urine of halal animals.
   Washing can clean Najasat Haqeqi on body or clothe by rinsing 3 times and squeezing.
2. **Hukmi** – Filth can't be seen such as: break of Wudu, need bath.

Istinja Masail: (Makruh- something against the conduct of Islam).
1. Use left hand only for Istenja.
2. It is Sunnah to make Wudu after urine, pass stool.
3. It is permissible to use tissue paper, toilet paper or dry earth for Istenja to clean private parts.
4. It is Makruh to use coal, bones, glass, baked bricks, and printed paper.
5. It is Makruh to urinate standing, face or show back towards Kaba when urinate or pass stool.
6. Remove rings, badges or anything with name of Allah, Rasul, Qur'anic verses or Hadith; they can be in the pocket.
7. Don't urinate or pass stool on road, under a tree or its shade, in a well, dam, river.
8. If you are in an open space without a toilet, use a place where no one can see you.

Enter Toilet with left foot and say:

اللّٰهُمَّ إِنِّى أَعُوْذُبِكَ مِنَ الْخُبْثِ وَالْخَبَائِثِ

Allahumma inni auzubeka minal khubuse wal khabaese.
(O Allah! I seek protection in you from male and female devil).

Leave toilet with right foot and say: غُفْرَانَكَ
Ghofranaka (I ask your forgiveness)

Steps to use Bathroom

1. Recite du'a to enter with left foot in first.
2. Clean seating area, put some tissue paper in toilet water to stop splash back upwards.
3. Squat (preferred) or sit on toilet.
4. After you finish, clean with tissue paper and use water to wash.
5. If you urinate, hold tissue paper at tip (for men), walk and cough to ensure last drop of urine come out and then wash with water.
6. Do not urinate standing.
7. Wash both places of private parts with water.
8. Clean seating area and flush toilet for next person to use.
9. Do not use napkin instead of tissue paper and do not throw napkin in water, as it will clog toilet.
10. Recite du'a to leave toilet with right foot out first.

Wudu / Ablution

Wudu means to wash hand, face, and leg, wipe head to make Salat or read Qur'an.

1. No Salat is acceptable to Allah without Wudu.
2. Wudu / Gusl is allowed with water from: rain, well, pond, spring, sea, river, melting snow.
3. Wudu / Gusl is not allowed with water from: unclean area, fruit and trees, water with changed color, taste, smell and thick with something soaked; small water with urine, blood, stool, wine, dead animal; used Wudu / Gusl water; water left over after drinking by haram animal such as dog, pig, animal of prey, water left by a person who drink wine.
4. It is Sunnah to make niyat for Wudu.
5. Sit on a high and clean place to make Wudu, face Kaba if possible.

Du'a before Wudu: بِسْمِ اللهِ وَالْحَمْدُ لِلّهِ
Bismillahe walhumdu lillah
(I begin with the name of Allah. And all praises are due to Allah).

Du'a during Wudu: اَللّهُمَّ اغْفِرْلِىْ ذَنْبِىْ وَوَسِّعْ لِى فِى دَارِىْ وَبَارِكْ لِى فِىْ رِزْقِىْ *Allahumughfirli zanbi wawassili fidari wabarikli fi rizki*
(O Allah! Forgive my sins and provide abundance in my home and grant me blessings in my sustenance).

Du'a after Wudu: اَشْهَدُ اَنْ لَآ اِلٰهَ اِلَّا اللهُ وَاَشْهَدُ اَنَّ مُحَمَّدًا عَبْدُهُ وَرَسُوْلُهُ

Ash-hadu allailaha illallahu wash-hadu anna muhammadun abduhu warasuluhu. (I testify that there is none worthy of worship but Allah and I testify that Muhammad ﷺ is Allah's worshipper and messenger).

اَللّٰهُمَّ اجْعَلْنِىْ مِنَ التَّوَّابِيْنَ وَاجْعَلْنِىْ مِنَ الْمُتَطَهِّرِيْنَ

Allahummuj alni minat tawabeena wajalni minul mutatahhirina
(O Allah! Make me of the repenters and make me of the purified).

4 Fard / Compulsory acts of Wudu: (Wudu is void if anyone is missed)

1. Wash face from forehead to lower chin and from one ear to the other.
2. Wash both arms including elbows.
3. Masah of quarter of head once.
4. Wash both feet including ankles once.

13 Sunnats of Wudu: (carry extra rewards)

1. Niyat / intention.
2. Recite bismillah.
3. Wash hands up to wrists 3 times.
4. Use meswak for teeth.
5. Gargle 3 times.
6. Run water into nostrils 3 times.
7. Khilal of beard.
8. Khilal of fingers and toes.
9. Wash each part 3 times.
10. Masah whole head once.
11. Masah both ears once.
12. Wudu is done systematically.
13. Wash each part one after another without pause so that no part dries up before Wudu is complete.

5 Mustahabs in Wudu: (carry extra rewards and no penalty if left out)

1. Begin from right.
2. Masah of nape.
3. Do not take help from anyone.
4. Face Qiblah.
5. Sit on high and clean place.

7 Wudu Steps

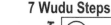

(1) **Hand:** Use clear water, wash both hands upto wrist 3 times

(2) It is Sunnah to use meswak (70 times more rewards) to clean teeth and Gargle mouth 3 times

(3) **Nose**: Run water upto nostrils 3 times with right hand and Clean nose with left hand.

(4) **Face**: Wash face 3 times – From hairline to below chin and From one ear to the other. Run water / khilal of beard.

(5) **Hands**: Wash right and left hand including elbows 3 times. Run water / khilal of fingers.

(6) **Masah**: Wet hands and pass them over the head, ears, and nape. This is done once. Keep 3 fingers of each hand together (middle, ring and little), keep thumb and index finger raised, and pass 3 fingers from forehead to upper nape. Place palm on sides of head and bring forward to forehead. Insert index finger into ears. Make masah behind ears with thumb. Make masah of nape with back of middle, ring and little fingers.

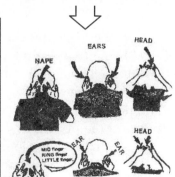

(7) **Feet.** Wash both feet including ankles 3 times- first right and then left including khalil of toes.

4 Makrohs: (Wudu is OK but with less reward)
1. Make Wudu in a dirty place.
2. Clean nose with right hand.
3. Talk worldly affairs.
4. Do Wudu against Sunnah.

Wudu Breaks if
1. Discharge urine, stool, anything from private parts.
2. Discharge gas.
3. Vomit in mouthful.
4. Fall sleepy lying down or resting body against something.
5. Faint.
6. Become insane or mad.
7. Laugh loud while in Salat.
8. Flow blood or matter from body.

Wudu Masail / Issues
1. If blood or matter does not move from place of wound or sore, Wudu will not break.
2. If clot of blood (not fluid state) come out of nose while blowing, Wudu will not break.
3. If a pimple busts in the eye and flows, or water flows due to eye pain, Wudu will break.
4. If blood in saliva is more than saliva, Wudu will break.
5. Blood on toothpick will not break Wudu if the blood cannot be seen in saliva.
6. Fluid from a paining ear will break Wudu even though there is no sore or pimple in ear.
7. If male falls sleep in sejda but does not topple over, Wudu will not break. If female falls sleep in sejda, Wudu will break.
8. A doubt whether Wudu is broken or not, will not make Wudu invalid.
9. During Wudu, if in doubt whether certain part was washed or not, only that part need to be washed. If such doubt occurs after Wudu, then Wudu is complete.
10. After Wudu, if one remembers certain part definitely not washed, then only that part need to be washed, repeat of whole Wudu in not necessary.
11. It is not permissible without Wudu to touch Qur'an, anything with Qur'anic verse written.

12. It is mustahab / preferable to make Wudu for each Salat even with Wudu state.

13. It is mustahab to perform at least 2 rakats Salat with a previous Wudu before a new Wudu is done unless Wudu is broken.

14. If 4 parts (Fard) of Wudu are soaked in rain, washed by swimming, bath, Wudu is valid even if one had no intention of Wudu.

15. It is makrooh to strike / splash water on the face.

16. It is makrooh (incomplete Wudu) to keep eyes closed while running water over eyes and prevent water to enter into eyes.

17. It is makrooh (incomplete Wudu) to close mouth while running water and some areas inside mouth remain dry.

18. Wudu is not valid if any substance such as gum, nail polish, paint cover the 4 parts (Fard) and water could not reach. If those substances are removed and washed with water, Wudu is valid. It is nor necessary to renew Wudu.

19. If removal of ointment from sore or wound is harmful, it is not necessary to remove it. If pouring water over affected area is harmful, then merely Masah over the area is sufficient.

20. If wound or sore is bandaged and is difficult to open and close and harmful, then Masah over the bandage is OK.

21. It is wajib to make Masah more than 50% of bandage otherwise Wudu is not valid.

22. After Masah over bandage, if it is loose and realized that affected part is healed, then Masah is not valid. Washing with water is necessary only on the affected area.

23. If the beard is thick then it is not Fard to reach water to beard skin. If beard grows thin, then it is Fard for water to reach skin as well.

24. Liquid from eye during yawning does not break Wudu.

25. Finger nails should be short. Dirt accumulates under long finger nails. Wudu and Gusl are invalid if water can not flow under long nails.

26. Odor from cigarette, cigar, raw onions is offensive. Mouth should be washed thoroughly after smoking.

Gusl / Bath

What Type of Water?

1. Water used in Wudu or Gusl (itself tahir / clean) can not be used again for Wudu or Gusl.
2. Water from which dog, pig, cat (after eating a mouse etc), animal of prey, and drunk man have drunk is impure.
3. Water left after drinking by cat (not eaten a mouse), cow, buffalo, hen, lizard, crow, hawk, eagle and all other haram birds is makrooh.
4. Water left over by human, halal animals e.g. goat, cow, dove is tahir / clean.
5. If najasat falls in water, water becomes unclean except flowing water of river / sea, stored water in large reservoir.
6. A large reservoir tank is defined as 21'x 21'and deep enough for a person to remove water by hand without touching ground.
7. Any animal or bird with flowing blood falls in small water and dies will make water unclean.
8. Water of a big tank becomes impure when taste, color, smell of najasat becomes apparent.
9. Anything alive (fish, frog) and die in water do not make water impure.

3 Fard of Gusl (Gusl is void if anyone is missed):

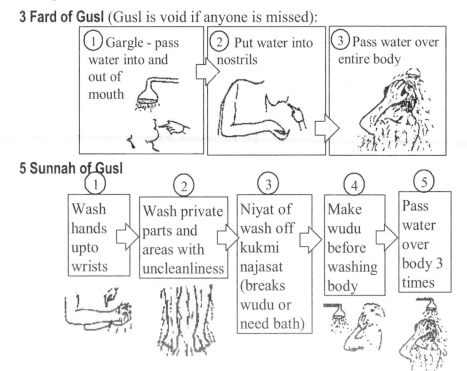

① Gargle - pass water into and out of mouth

② Put water into nostrils

③ Pass water over entire body

5 Sunnah of Gusl

①	②	③	④	⑤
Wash hands upto wrists	Wash private parts and areas with uncleanliness	Niyat of wash off kukmi najasat (breaks wudu or need bath)	Make wudu before washing body	Pass water over body 3 times

Rules during Gusl: Gusl should be made
1. In a private place.
2. Without facing Qiblah.
3. Standing or preferably seating.
4. Without skimp or waste water.
5. Without talk.
6. Without reciting Kalima or Qur'an. Niyat should be made before Gusl. Without Niyat, there is no reward though Gusl is valid.

Gusl Procedure
1. Wash both hands including wrists.
2. Wash hands, private parts even if not in janabat or najasat.
3. Perform Wudu.
4. Pour water over head 3 times.
5. Pour water 3 times over right shoulder and 3 times over left shoulder.
6. Pour water over entire body and rub. It is mustahab to clean by rubbing.
7. It is compulsory to wet all hair of head. If a single hair is left dry, Gusl is not valid.
8. Women are excused from loosening hair but compulsory to wet the base of each hair otherwise Gusl is not valid.
9. Rings, earrings should be removed to ensure that no portion covered is left dry. Naval and ears must be wet.
10. Dry body with clean towel and dress quickly.
11. After Gusl, if one remembers certain area is left dry, wash that dry area. It is not necessary to repeat Gusl.

Gusl Masail / Issues
1. It is OK to wash body and not head if harmful due to sickness.
2. Cover body with clothes quickly after Gusl.
3. It is not necessary to remove ointment from wound. Just pour water over it.
4. After Gusl, Wudu is not necessary.
5. It is preferable to cut nails, toes, and remove hair from under armpits and below the navel area before bath. They should be removed within every 40 days. Clipping sequence of fingers is: right index to right little, then from left little to left thumb and then right thumb. Toe nails from right small and end with left small.

Hand nail clipping sequence	Toe nail clipping sequence
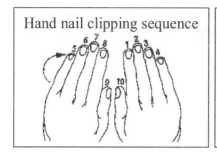	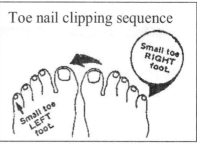

6. It is compulsory to perform Gusl in the state of janabat (impurity).

7. It is compulsory for women to have bath after haij (monthly menstruation period) and nifas (40 days after childbirth or when blood flow stops).

Tayamum and Masah of Socks

Tayamum is to use clean earth or clay instead of Wudu to get rid of najasat hukmiya (need bath or Wudu).

Tayamum is permitted under the following Conditions

1. Water is not available within one-mile radius.
2. Use of water would definitely harm health.
3. Fear of enemy or dangerous animal or snake near water.
4. Water is so little that if used for Wudu or Gusl, there is fear of thirst.
5. No rope or bucket is available to pull water from well or can not reach water nearby or no one is available to fetch water.
6. One does not have sufficient money to pay for water being sold.
7. If water is sold at a very ridiculous price.
8. It is not necessary to fetch water if there is no trace of water, no information regarding water around, water may be found after a mile.
9. If so little water is available that 4 Fard of Wudu can be performed then Tayamum is not permitted.
10. If najis / filth has fallen on ground or sand, then that ground can not be used for Tayamum even if it is dry.
11. If body is najis / unclean and little water is available, then use water to clean najasat from body and clothes and then perform Tayamum.

Fard of Tayamum (Tayamum is void if anyone is missed)

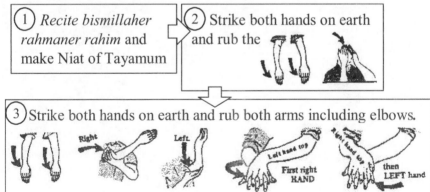

1. *Recite bismillaher rahmaner rahim* and make Niat of Tayamum
2. Strike both hands on earth and rub the
3. Strike both hands on earth and rub both arms including elbows.

Right   Left

Left hand top   First right HAND

then LEFT hand

Masnoon / preferred Tayamum Procedure

1. First recite *bismillaher rahmaner rahim* and make niyat of Tayamum in exchange of Gusl or Wudu.
2. Strike both hands on earth or dust, blow off excess dust on hands, rub both hands over complete face without leaving any space.
3. Strike both hands on ground, blow off excess dust, rub left hand over complete right hand including elbow, rub right hand over complete left hand including elbow.
4. Remove ring if any. Do Khilal of fingers, beard (Sunnah).

Tayamum Masail

1. Tayamum is permitted on clean earth, sand, stone, limestone, baked earth pots, walls of mud, stone or brick, clay, item with thick dust on it. Stone, brick or clay pot does not need to be with dust to use.
2. Tayamum is not permitted on wood, metal, glass, food items, item burned to ash or rot or melt.
3. Tayamum is allowed for Janaza or Eid Salat (they do not have qaza).
4. It is not necessary to repeat Salat with Tayamum if water is found later. Duration of Tayamum is as long as water is not available or sick. It can be for years even.

Tayamum breaks if

1. Things which break Wudu also break Tayamum.
2. Tayamum for Gusl breaks only after Fard Gusl is needed.
3. Tayamum breaks when water is found.
4. Tayamum done due to disease breaks if cured.
5. One can perform any number of Salat with one Tayamum as long as it does not break.
6. Tayamum for Fard Salat is valid for Nafl, reading Qur'an, all other Salats.

Masah of Kuffain / Socks

Kuffain is special type of socks. Instead of washing feet during Wudu, it is permissible to pass moist hands / Masah over such socks.

Types of Socks for Masah: (If any of these 4 conditions is missing, Masah is not valid):
1. Socks must be strong enough to walk on roads 3 miles without tearing.
2. Socks should remain in position without tying, do not slip.
3. Water can not seep through.
4. Socks not transparent.

Masah Masail / Issues
1. Kuffain is generally made of leather. Any material, which meets above 4 conditions, is allowed. Sock made of wool, nylon are not Kuffain.
2. Kuffain should be worn after first complete Wudu including foot wash. After that Masah on Kuffain can be done instead of foot wash during any subsequent Wudu. Kuffain can be used up to 24 hours for local person (not traveling) and 72 hours for traveler. Thereafter, Kuffain should be removed, new Wudu with feet wash with water is required and then Kuffain can be worn again.

Masah Procedure
1. Draw fingers of right hand on upper surface of Kuffain starting from toes to foreleg just before ankle. Same with left hand fingers on left leg. Masah should be done once on each sock.
2. It is not required to make Masah on the side or under surface of Kuffain. It is Fard to make Masah on each sock with 3 full fingers.
3. Masah is void if sock is removed, things happen which nullify Wudu, Masah period expires (24 hours for local, 72 hours for travel).

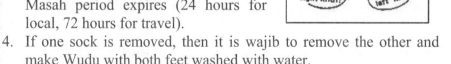

Masah Procedure

Right hand right khuff   Left hand left khuff

4. If one sock is removed, then it is wajib to remove the other and make Wudu with both feet washed with water.
5. If lowering sock exposes foreleg, it will be considered as the whole sock is removed and void Masah.

6. Masah on torn sock with the size of 3 small toes exposed is void.
7. If seam of sock comes loose but foot is not exposed during walking, Masah is OK.
8. If a local person with Masah goes on journey before expiry of 24 hours, Masah period will be extended to 72 hours.
9. It is OK to Masah on ordinary woolen socks, which is covered with leather.
10. If Gusl becomes compulsory, Masah is not valid even the period has not yet expired. Kuffain must be removed during Gusl and feet washed.
11. If after Masah, foot falls in water with more than 50% foot is wet, Masah is invalid. Both Kuffain must be removed and feet washed.

Chapter – 3: Azan + Salat and Salat Conditions

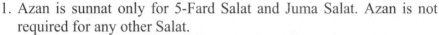

Azan / Call towards Salat

1. Azan is sunnat only for 5-Fard Salat and Juma Salat. Azan is not required for any other Salat.
2. Azan of every Fard Salat should be called out in its prescribed time. If it is called before time starts, it must be called again at the correct time.
3. Calling azan without Wudu is permissible but is not a good habit.
4. The person who calls Azan is called **Moazzin**. Moazzin stands up and calls out loudly facing Qiblah these words with his ears closed by fingers:

---

① **Facing** Qibla:

4 Times: اَللهُ اَكْبَرُ

Allahu akbar (Allah is the Greatest of all)

2 Times: اَشْهَدُ اَنْ لآاِلهَ اِلاَّ اللهُ

Ash-haduanla ilaha illallah

(I testify that there is none worthy of worship but Allah)

2 Times: اَشْهَدُ اَنَّ مُحَمَّدًا رَسُوْلُ اللهِ

Ashadu anna muhammadar rasulullah

(I testify that Muhammad ﷺ is Allah's Messenger)

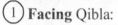

---

② **Turning Face to** Right:

2 Times: حَىَّ عَلَى الصَّلوةِ

haia aalas salat

(Come for Salat)

③ **Turning Face to** Left:

2 Times: حَىَّ عَلَى الْفَلاَح

haia aalul falah

(Come for Success)

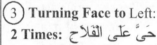

---

④ **Turning Face** Back to Qibla:

> **For Fajr Salat only:**
> **2 Times:** اَلصَّلوةُ خَيْرٌ مِّنَ النَّوْم
> *Assalatu kharirum minun naoom*
> (The salat is better than sleep)

2 Times: اَللهُ اَكْبَرُ

Allahu akbar (Allah is the Greatest of all)

1 Time: لاَ اِلهَ اِلاَّ اللهُ

la ilaha illallah (There is none worthy of worship besides Allah)

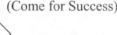

Du'a After Azan

اَللَّهُمَّ رَبَّ هَذِهِ الدَّعْوَةِ التَّامَّةِ وَالصَّلَاةِ الْقَائِمَةِ اتِ مُحَمَّدًا الْوَسِيْلَةَ وَالْفَضِيْلَةَ وَابْعَثْهُ
مَقَامًا مَحْمُوْدًا الَّذِيْ وَعَدْتَهُ إِنَّكَ لَاتُخْلِفُ الْمِيَعَادِ

allahumma rabba Hazihid dawatet tammate wassalawatel qaemate aate muhammada nilwasilata walfadilata wabas-hu maqamam mahmooda nillazi waadtahu innaka la tukhleful miad. (O Allah! Lord of this perfect call and of the Salat about to be established bestow upon Muhammad sallalahu alaihe wasallam the wasilah (intercession), Grace and the lofty rank. Place him on Makame Mahmud, which You have promised him. Verily, You do not go against the promise).

7 Mustahabs in Azan

1. Stand facing Qiblah.
2. Don't haste in saying Azan.
3. Put both index fingers in both ears (one each).
4. Call azan from a high place.
5. Say azan in a loud voice.
6. Turn face *right* and say 2 times: haia alas Salat, Turn face left and say 2 times: haia alal falah.
7. Say 2 times: *Assalatu khairum minun naoom* after haia alal falah in the azan for **Fajr** Salat.

Iqamat / Call Just before Salat Starts

Iqamat means: Repeat of azan words before Fard Salat starts.
Say twice after haia alal falah. قَدْقَامَتِ الصَّلوةُ
Qadqamatis Salat (Prayer is ready)

1. The person who calls Iqamat is called **Mukabbir**.
2. Saying Iqamat without Wudu is makrooh.
3. Azan and Iqamat is Sunnah for men only and for Fard Salat only. They are not necessary for any other Salat.
4. You should say azan and Iqamat at home, or travel even alone when you pray Fard Salat. It is OK to say Iqamat and not Azan. It is Makruh to leave both.
5. It is OK if one person says azan and another person says Iqamat but it will be Makruh to do without permission.
6. It is recommended to wait sufficiently after azan is called for people to come before Iqamat is called except Maghrib Salat which should start after time to recite 3 ayats / sentences of Qur'an is passed.

Ijabat / Repeat of Azan and Iqamat Words

1. Repeat of the words of azan and Iqamat is called **Ijabat**. It is mustahab. Anyone hears Moazzin or Mukabbir should also pronounce quietly.

2. During haia alas Salat and haia alal falah, one should say:

لاَحَوْلَ وَلاَ قُوَةَ اِلاَّ بِاللهِ ال عَلَى الْعَظِيْم

Lahowla wala quwwata illabillahel aliul azim. (There is no power and might except from Allah. The most High –The Great)

3. In Fajr Salat Azan, during *Assalatu khairum minun naoom*, one should say: صَدَقْتَ وَبَرَرْتَ

sadaqta wabararta.

(You have spoken the truth and you have done good)

4. During qadqamatis Salat, one should say: أَقَامَهَا اللهُ وَادَامَهَا

aqamaha allahu wadamaha.

(May Allah establish it and keep it forever)

Salat / Prayer

- After Iman / faith, most important order of Allah is Salat. If someone took good care of Salat, Allah will relax judgment for that person. That is why it is very important that Salat is performed correctly and on time.
- Before Salat: ensure clothes are clean, make Wudu, stand respectfully on clean place, face Qiblah, keep feet parallel, and submit to Allah.

Salat Dress
Men: no garment or trousers should overlap ankles. It is makrooh to overlap and so rewards will be much less.

Women: same as men except: hands not exposed, raise hands to shoulder height when say Allah Akbar.

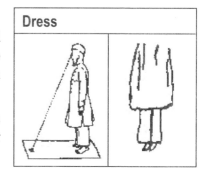

Dress

Salat Steps:
1. **Niyat:** Make niyat for whichever Salat you are performing with number of rakats. If you pray in jamat, say I follow imam. It is not necessary to say verbally. Niyat can be made in *any language*.

2. **Takbir Tahrima:** Lift two hands up to earlobs (for men) or up to shoulders (for women) with both palms face Qiblah, say *Allahu Akbar*. Fold both palms with right hand over the back of left hand with right thumb and little finger holding the wrist of the left hand and three middle fingers of right hand kept straight and together.

Takbire Tahrima

Both palms should be below the navel (for men) and over the chest (for women). Eyes during standing should be on a fixed point at sejda.

3. Thana + Tawuz + Tasmia

Thana: سُبْحَانَكَ اللّهُمَّ وَبِحَمْدِكَ وَتَبَارَكَ اسْمُكَ وَتَعَالَى جَدُّكَ وَلاَ اِلهَ غَيْرُكَ

subhanaka allahumma wabehumdeka watabara kasmuka wataala jadduka walailaha ghairuka. (All glory be to you O Allah! And praise is to you. Blessed is Your name and Exalted is Your Majesty, and there is none worthy of worship besides You).

Tawwuz: اَعُوْذُ بِاللهِ مِنَ الشَّيْطَانِ الرَّجِيْمِ

auzubillahe minash shaitaner rajim. (I seek refuge in Allah from Satan the Accused).

Tasmia: بِسْمِ اللهِ الرَّحْمَنِ الرَّحِيْمِ

bismillaher rahmaner rahim. (In the name of Allah, the Most Gracious, the Most Merciful).

First Rakat Starts...

4. Follow 4a, 4b, 4c depending on type of Salat listed in Table. Last 10 Suras are listed in Chapter-9.

4a. Sura Fateha + any Sura (loudly)	4b. Sura Fateha + any Sura (silently)	4c. Sura Fateha only (silently)

5. Ruku

Ruku

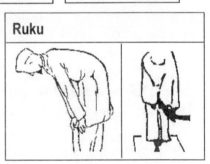

Say *allahu akbar* اللهُ اَكْبَرُ (Allah is Great) and go to Ruku. **Men:** Hold both knees with fingers apart. Ensure that arms do not touch body. Keep back straight, head is neither lowered or raised.

Women: Bend sufficiently to place hands on knees, Fingers kept together. Elbows should touch sides of body and feet kept together.

During Ruku recite softly at least 3 or 5 times. سُبْحَانَ رَبِّىَ الْعَظِيْمِ
subhana rabbial azim (How Glorious is my Lord the Great)

6. Tasme + Qawma + Tahmi

While standing up after Ruku, say سَمِعَ اللهُ لِمَنْ حَمِدَه
Tasme: *sami allah huleman hamida.* (Allah has listened to him who has praised Him).

Qawma: To stand up Straight.

If one does not stand straight after Ruku and goes to Sejda, then Salat is void and must be repeated.

Tahmid: During upright position, say: رَبَّنَا وَلَكَ الْحَمْدُ
rabbana lakal hamdu. (O our Lord! Praise be to You).

7. First Sejda

Say *allahu akbar* اللهُ اكْبَرُ
(should be completed by Sejda).
Place both hands on knees, first
place knees on ground, then
hands on ground, then nose and
then
forehead to go to Sejda. Follow
reverse order when getting up
from Sejda. Face should rest
between two hands with fingers
pointing towards qibla.
Feet should be upright with toes pointing towards the Qiblah and
touching ground. Feet should not be lifted. Arms should not touch
sides of body nor the ground. Stomach should be away from thighs.
Women: Thigh should be as flat position as possible, with feet
spread towards the right. Stomach and thighs must be kept together.
Forearms are placed flat on ground. Must not raise voice when
reciting tasbih.
During Sejda, recite softly at least 3 or 5 times…سُبْحَانَ رَبِّىَ الأعْلَى
subhana rabbial aala. (All Glory be to my Lord, the Most High)

8. **Jalsa** (sit between 2 sejdas):
Say *allahu akbar* and sit up
straight fully, pause after
first Sejda.
Men: Sit on left foot on
ground in flat position with
right foot upright, toe face
Qibla. Hands are placed on
thighs with finger tips close
together towards Qibla.
Eyes are fixed on the lap.
Women: Sit on ground,
both legs lay flat on side.

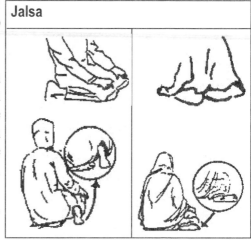

9. Second Sejda

Second Sejda is performed like the First sejda.
Say *allahu akbar*, go to ground, say tasbih *subhana rabbial aala* at least 3 times. After Second Sejda, one rakat cycle is completed.

10. Stand up

Say *allahu akbar* الله اكْبَرُ and stand up for next Rakat

Second Rakat Starts………..Follow Steps 4, 5, 6, 7, 8, 9

11A. First Qaida

After second Sejda of second rakat, say *allahu akbar* الله اكْبَرُ and sit for Qaida. Sitting positions are same as those of Jalsa. Read Tasahud:

First Qaida / Tashahud

اَلتَّحِيَّاتُ لِلّهِ وَالصَّلَوتُ وَالطَّيِّبَاتُ اَلسَّلَامُ عَلَيْكَ اِيُّهَا النَّبِىُّ وَرَحْمَةُ اللهِ وَبَرَكَاتُه
اَلسَّلَامُ عَلَيْنَا وَعَلَى عِبَادِ اللهِ الصَّلِحِيْنَ اَشْهَدُ اَنْ لاَاِلهَ اِلاَّ اللهُ وَاَشْهَدُ اَنَّ مُحَمَّدًا
عَبْدُه وَرَسُوْلُه

Attahiatu lillahe wassalawatu wattaiyebatu assalamu alaika ayyuhun nabiu warahmatullahe wabarakatuhu. assalamu alaina waala ebadillahes saaliheen. Ash-hadu allailaha illallahu wash-hadu anna muhammadan abduhu warasuluhu.(All reverence, all worship, all sanctity are due to Allah. Peace be upon you O Prophet ﷺ, and the mercy of Allah and His blessings. Peace be upon us and all the righteous servants of Allah. I bear witness that none is worthy of worship besides Allah and Muhammad ﷺ is His devotee and Messenger).

When reciting Kalema اَشْهَدُ اَنْ لاَاِلهَ *ash-hadu allailaha illallahu*, form a circle with the thumb and middle finger and lift index finger of the right hand and at *illallahu*, drop it onto the thigh. The circle should be maintained to the end.

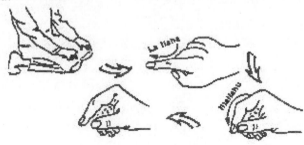

Third Rakat Starts ………..Follow Steps 4, 5, 6, 7, 8, 9

Fourth Rakat Starts ………Follow Steps 4, 5, 6, 7, 8, 9

11B. Second Qaida

In the Second Qaida, after Tashahud read Durude Ibrahim:

Second Qaida + Du'a (optional)

اَللّٰهُمَّ صَلِّ عَلٰى مُحَمَّدٍ وَّعَلٰى الِ مُحَمَّدٍ كَمَا صَلَّيْتَ عَلٰى اِبْرٰهِيْمَ وَعَلٰى الِ اِبْرٰهِيْمَ

اِنَّكَ حَمِيْدٌ مَّجِيْدٌ اَللّٰهُمَّ بَارِكْ عَلٰى مُحَمَّدٍ وَّعَلٰى الِ مُحَمَّدٍ كَمَا بَارَكْتَ عَلٰى اِبْرٰهِيْمَ

وَعَلٰى الِ اِبْرٰهِيْمَ اِنَّكَ حَمِيْدٌ مَّجِيْدٌ

Allahumma salleala muhammadeu waala ale muhammadin kama sallaita ala ibrahima waala ale ibrahima innaka hamidum majid. allahumma barek alaa muhammadeu waala ale muhammadin kama barakta ala ibrahima waala ale ibrahima innaka hamidum majid. (O Allah! Shower Your mercy upon Muhammad 鬱 and the followers of Muhammad 鬱, as You showered Your mercy upon Ibrahim and the followers of Ibrahim. Behold, You are praiseworthy, glorious, O Allah! Shower Your blessings upon Muhammad 鬱 and the followers of Muhammad 鬱, as You showered Your blessings upon Ibrahim and the followers of Ibrahim. Behold, You are praiseworthy, glorious).

Du'a after Durud (optional)

اَللّٰهُمَّ اِنِّى ظَلَمْتُ نَفْسِى ظُلْمًا كَثِيْرًا وَّلَا يَغْفِرُ الذُّنُوْبَ اِلَّا أَنْتَ فَاغْفِرْلِى مَغْفِرَةً مِنْ

عِنْدِكَ وَارْحَمْنِىْ اِنَّكَ أَنْتَ الْغَفُوْرُ الرَّحِيْمُ

Allahumma inni zalamtu nafsi zulmun kasirao wainnahu la yaghferu zunuba illaanta fughfirli mughferatum minendeka warhumni innaka antal ghafurur rahim. (O Allah! I have been extremely unjust to myself, and none grants forgiveness against sins but You; forgive me with forgiveness that comes from You, and have Mercy upon me. Verily You are the Forgiving, the Merciful).

12. Du'a Qunut

اَللّٰهُمَّ اِنَّا نَسْتَعِيْنُكَ وَنَسْتَغْفِرُكَ وَنُؤْمِنُ بِكَ وَنَتَوَكَّلُ عَلَيْكَ وَنُثْنِىْ عَلَيْكَ الْخَيْرَ

وَنَشْكُرُكَ وَلَانَكْفُرُكَ وَنَخْلَعُ وَنَتْرُكُ مَنْ يَّفْجُرُكَ اَللّٰهُمَّ اِيَّاكَ نَعْبُدُ وَلَكَ نُصَلِّىْ وَنَسْجُدُ

وَاِلَيْكَ نَسْعٰى وَنَحْفِدُ وَنَرْجُوْ رَحْمَتَكَ وَنَخْشٰى عَذَابَكَ اِنَّ عَذَابَكَ بِالْكُفَّارِ مُلْحِقٌ

Allahumma inna nastaenuka wanastugh feruka wanumenu beka wanata-wakkalu alaika wanusne alaikal khair. wanashkuruka wala nakfuruka wanakhlau wanatruku maiyaf juruka. allahumma iyaka

nabudu walaka nusalli wanasjudu wailaika nasa wanahfezu wanarju rahmataka wanakhsha azabaka inna azabaka bilkuffare mulhiq.
(O Allah: we beseech Your help and we ask Your Pardon and we believe in You and we put our trust in You and we praise You in the best manner and we thank You and we are not ungrateful to You and we cast off, and leave one who disobeys You. O Allah: You alone we serve and to You de we pray and we prostrate and to You do we flee and we are quick and we hope for Your mercy and we fear Your punishment. No doubt Your punishment overtakes the unbelievers).

13. Salam
Turn face to RIGHT saying

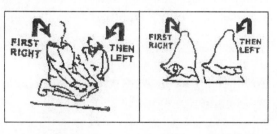

ٱلسَّلَامُ عَلَيْكُمْ وَرَحْمَةُ اللهِ

assalamu alaikum warahmatulla. (Peace be upon you and the mercy of Allah).Then turn face to

LEFT and repeat salam. Eyes should be fixed on respective shoulders.

Completion of Salat
Recite أَسْتَغْفِرُ ا اللهِ

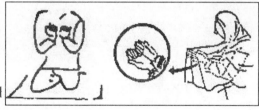

Astaghfirullah 3 times.
Raise both hands to chest level and make Du'a to Allah

Du'as after Salat

There are various Du'as. You can ask your needs to Allah through these Du'as or your own in your own language.

رَبَّنَا اتِنَا فِى الدُّنْيَا حَسَنَةً وَّفِى الاخِرَةِ حَسَنَةً وَّقِنَا عَذَابَ النَّارِ

rabbana atena fidduniya hasanatawn wafil akherate hasanatao waqina azabunnar. (O Allah! Grant us in the world virtue and in the hereafter virtue and protect us from the punishment of the fire).

رَبَّنَا تَقَبَّلْ مِنَّا اِنَّكَ اَنْتَ السَّمِيْعُ الْعَلِيْمُ وَتُبْ عَلَيْنَا اِنَّكَ اَنْتَ التَّوَّابُ الرَّحِيْمُ

rabbana taqabbal minna innaka antas samiul alim. (Our Rabb accept from us (this duty). Definitely you only are the Hearer, the Knower).

اَللهُمَّ اَعِنَّا عَلَى ذِكْرِكَ وَشُكْرِكَ وَحُسْنِ عِبَادَتِكَ

allahumma aainna ala zikrika washukrika wahusne ebadatik. (O Allah, help us in remembering You and being grateful to You and worshipping You well)

اللَّهُمَّ أَنْتَ السَّلامُ وَمِنْكَ السَّلامُ تَبَارَكْتَ يَاذَا الْجَلالِ وَالإِكْرَامِ

allahumma antas salam waminkas salam tabarakta yazaljalale walikram. (O Allah! You are safe and from You we receive safety. You are Blessed, Lofty and Dignified).

سُبْحَانَ رَبِّكَ رَبِّ الْعِزَّةِ عَمَّا يَصِفُوْنَ وَسَلامٌ عَلَىْ الْمُرْسَلِيْنَ وَالْحَمْدُ لِلّهِ رَبِّ الْعلمِيْنَ

subhana rabbika rabbil ezzate amma yasefun wasalamun alal mursalin walhamdu lillahe rabbil aalamin. (Glorified is our Lord, the Lord of Honor above what they describe, and Salam on the Messengers. And all praise to Allah, the Lord of the worlds).

Conditions and Rules of Salat

Fard of Salat

There are 13 Fard / Compulsory conditions of Salat. 7 are before Salat is started and 6 are inside Salat. If any of these conditions are missed, Salat will not be accepted or considered void.

7 Compulsory Conditions *before* Salat can be started are

1. Body Clean (free from filth and impurities - make Wudu for Haqeqi najasat such as urine, blood, stool, wine; Hukmi Najasat which can not be seen; or Gusl if compulsory due to Janabah)
2. Clean Dress
3. Cover Satr (Male's satr is from navel to below (including) knee, Female's satr is entire body except face and hands to the wrist).
4. Clean place.
5. Face Qibla (direction of Kaba)
6. Niyat for Salat
7. Perform Salat at prescribed time.

6 Compulsory Conditions *Inside* Salat are

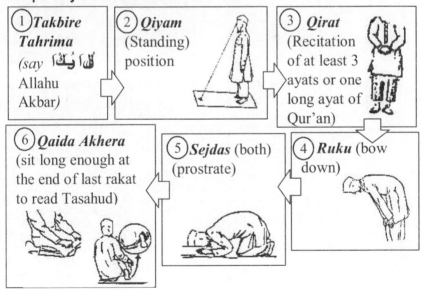

Types of Salats and Their Requirements

5 Daily Salats	Time Range *	Total Rakats	Sunnat	Fard	Sunnat	Nafl	Witr	Nafl	Comments
Fajr	Early Dawn to before Sunrise	4	2 (Muakkada)	2					
Zuhr	Past noon to twice the shadow of object + original shadow at Zawal	12	4 (Muakkada)	4	2 (Muakkada)	2 (Optional)			
Asr	Zuhr finish time to before Sunset.	8	4 (Muakkada)	4					
Maghrib	After Sunset to when redness fades.	7		3	2	2 (Optional)			
Isa	After redness disappears (about 1.5 hours after sunset) to before Dawn.	17	4 (Muakkada)	4	2	2 (Optional)	3	2 (Optional)	It is Mustahab to perform before 1/3rd of night has passed. It is Makrooh to delay after midnight.
Juma (Friday)	Same as for Zuhr	14	4	2	4	2		2 (Optional)	No Zuhr after Juma
Eid (Fitr and Azha)	After Sunrise to before Zawal	2		2					No Azan, no Iqamat, no Nafl before and after Eid. 2 rakats Wajib with 6 extra Takbirs (*Allahu Akbar*)

| Tarawih (Ramadan) | After Isa during Ramadan | 20 | | | | | | | | It is Sunnate Muakkada for men and women during Ramadan. Tarawih is after Isa Fard and sunnat. 2 rakats at a time. Witr is at the end. |
| Janaza (Funeral) | Any time except forbidden times | | | | | | | | | No Azan, no Iqamat, no rakats, 4 Takbirs only |

*Time vary from place to place and at different seasons.

Steps in Different Types of Salats

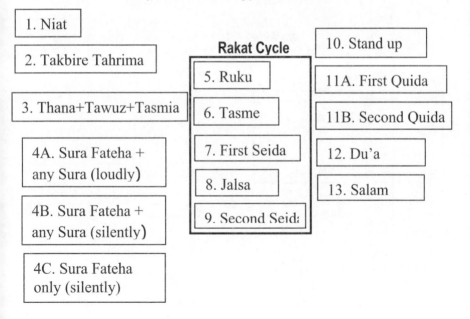

1. Niat

2. Takbire Tahrima

3. Thana+Tawuz+Tasmia

4A. Sura Fateha + any Sura (loudly)

4B. Sura Fateha + any Sura (silently)

4C. Sura Fateha only (silently)

Rakat Cycle

5. Ruku

6. Tasme

7. First Seida

8. Jalsa

9. Second Seida

10. Stand up

11A. First Quida

11B. Second Quida

12. Du'a

13. Salam

A = 2 Rakat Fard
B = 2 Rakat Sunnat / Nafl
C = 3 Rakat Fard @ Maghrib
D = 3 Rakat Witr @ Isa
E = 4 Rakat Fard @ Isa
F = 4 Rakat Fard @ Zuhr and Asr
G = 4 Rakat Sunnat / Nafl

A = 1+2+3+4A+(5-9)+10+4A+(5-9)+11A+11B+13
B = 1+2+3+4B+(5-9)+10+4B+(5-9)+11A+11B+13
C = 1+2+3+4A+(5-9)+10+4A+(5-9)+11A+10+4C+(5-9)
    +11A+11B+13
D = 1+2+3+4B+(5-9)+10+4B+(5-9)+11A+10+4B+2+12+(5-9)
    +11A+11B+13
E = 1+2+3+4A+(5-9)+10+4A+(5-9)+11A+10+4C+(5-9) +10+4C+
    (5-9)+11A+11B+13
F = 1+2+3+4B+(5-9)+10+4B+(5-9)+11A+10+4C+(5-9) +10+4C+
    (5-9)+11A+11B+13
G = 1+2+3+4B+(5-9)+10+4B+(5-9)+11A+10+4B+(5-9) +10+4B+
    (5-9)+11A+11B+13

Fajr	= B+A
Zohr	= G+F+B+B
Asr	= G+F
Magrib	= C+B+B
Isa	= G+E+B+B+D+B

Juma	= G+2 Khutbas+A+G+B+B
Eid	= A with 6 Extra Takbirs+2 Khutbas
Tarawih	= B+Durud+B+Tarawih Du'a,
	repeat 5 times = 20 rakats
Janaza	= 1+2+3+2+Durud+2+Janaza Du'a+2+13

Salat Times

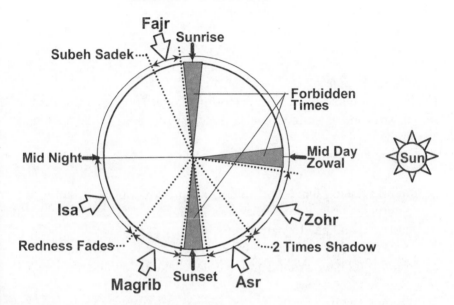

Forbidden Times of Salat (in 24 hours)

1. During sunrise.
2. During Zawal (when sun has reached highest point).
3. No Nafl Salat after Fajr Salat up to about 15 minutes after sunrise.
4. No Nafl Salat between Asr and Maghrib except Qaza and Janaza.
5. During sunset.

14 Wajib / Necessary in Salat: (If any one is missed unknowingly, Sejda Sahu (extra Sejda) can compensate, otherwise satat must be repeated)

1. Recite Qur'an in first 2 rakats of Fard Salat.
2. Recite Sura Fateha in all rakats of every Salat except 3rd and 4th rakats of Fard Salat.
3. Recite Sura after Sura Fateha in first 2 rakats of Fard Salat and in all other Salat.
4. Recite Sura Fateha before any other Sura.
5. Maintain order between qirat, Ruku, sejda and rakat.
6. Stand up after Ruku.
7. Sit between 2 sejdas.
8. Perform Ruku, sejda in good manner.
9. Sit to say *Tasahud* after 2 rakats in Salat of 3 or 4 rakats.

10. Recite *Tasahud* in 2 sittings.
11. Recite Qur'an loudly in Fajr, Maghrib, Isa, Juma, Eid, Tarawih Salat during Ramadan by Imam and silently at Zuhr and Asr.
12. To end Salat by saying *Salam*.
13. Say *Allahu Akbar* in Qunut in Witr Salat and recite du'a Qunut.
14. Say 6 additional Takbir in both Eid Salat.

21 Sunnats in Salat
(Nabi Muhammad ﷺ used to perform in Salat and carry extra rewards but if any one is missed, Salat is still valid and Sejda Sahu is not required)
1. Raise hands up to ears before saying Takbire Tahrima (Allahu Akbar).
2. While raising hands for Takbir, keep fingers of both hands raised and face Qibla.
3. Do not bend head when saying Takbir.
4. Say Takbire Tahrima and other Takbir loudly by Imam.
5. Fold right hand around and over left hand below the naval.
6. Say Sana.
7. Recite Tawuz.
8. Recite Bismillaher Rahmaner Rahim.
9. Recite only Sura Fateha in the 3rd and 4th rakats of Fard Salat.
10. Say Amin softly.
11. Recite Sana, Tawuz, Amin softly.
12. Recite as much qirat as in sunnat.
13. Say tasbih at least 3 times in each Ruku and sejda.
14. Keep Back and Head in the same level while holding Knees with Fingers in Ruku.
15. Say rabbana lakal hamd as Muqtadi after Imam says samiallahu liman hamida after Ruku during standing position.
16. While going to Sejda, first place Knees, then Hands and lastly Forehead on the ground.
17. In Qaida / Sitting, place Foot on ground horizontally, sit upon it and raise right foot vertically so that toes face Qibla, rest both hands on thighs.
18. Raise index finger of right hand when say ashadu allailaha in Tasahud.
19. Recite Durud sarif in last Qaida / sitting after Tasahud.
20. Read du'a after Durud sarif.
21. Turn face for Salam towards right first and the to left.

5 Mustahabs in Salat: (Carry extra rewards, no penalty if missed).
1. Pull palms out of sleeves while saying Takbire Tahrima.
2. Say tasbih more than 3 times in Ruku, sejda.
3. Keep eyes towards sejda place while standing, at toes in Ruku, towards lap in Qaida, at shoulders while turning for Salam.
4. Try not to cough.
5. Keep mouth closed when yawning, but if it is opened, cover it by upper portion of right hand in qiyam and by left hand in all other postures.

Makrooh / Undesirable acts in Salat
(Loose many reward if done, Salat don't need to repeat)
1. Say Salat bareheaded (not covered), expose arms above elbows.
2. Play with clothes or body.
3. Perform Salat in clothes which people do not like to go out.
4. Dust floor with hand to prevent soiling of clothes.
5. Perform Salat with pressure to urinate or pass stool.
6. Crack fingers or put fingers of one hand into fingers of other hand.
7. Turn face away from Qibla and look around.
8. To rest (for men only) both arms and wrists on the ground in sejda.
9. Perform Salat when another person facing him sits ahead.
10. Yawn intentionally and not prevent it.
11. Close eyes except for concentration.
12. A mature person to stand alone behind a row when there is place in the line before him.
13. Perform Salat in clothes with pictures of living objects on them.
14. Perform Salat at a place with picture of a living object.
15. To count ayats, Suras or tasbih on fingers in Salat.
16. Perform Salat with a sheet or clothes wrapped on a body in such way that it makes it difficult to free hands quickly.
17. To yawn and stretch arms to remove laziness.
18. Do something against sunnat in Salat.

Mufsidat / Breakers of Salat

(Nullify Salat if done during Salat and Salat must be repeated).

1. Talk knowingly or unknowingly.
2. Greet a person with Assalamu alaikum.
3. Reply to greetings or say yarhamukumullah to one's sneeze or say Amin to a du'a.
4. Say inna lillah on sad news or alhamdulillah on good news.
5. Make noise or say Oh or Aah due to pain.
6. Correct qirat / recitation of a person other than his own Imam in Salat.
7. Recite Qur'an by looking at the text.
8. Do such acts to create impression of acts other than Salat.
9. Eat or drink knowingly or unknowingly.
10. Turn chest away from qibla without excuse.
11. Perform sejda at a najis / dirty place.
12. Delay in covering satr when uncovered.
13. Talk in pain or trouble.
14. Laugh loud.
15. Step ahead of Imam during Salat.
16. Make big error during Qur'an recitation.

Conditions Allow Breaking Salat

1. Urge / pressure to pass urine or stool.
2. See harmful creature such as snake, scorpion.
3. Afraid that train will depart and cause inconvenience.
4. Afraid that thief will get away with shoes or any other property.
5. Answer (wajib) call of parent or grandparent who is in distress. It is not necessary if someone is around to assist.
6. It is Fard to break Salat in order to stop a blind person who might fall in a pit or well.
7. Help a person caught on fire.

Benefits of Salat with Jamat

1. Salat with jamat is 27 times greater in rewards than that performed alone. Jamat consists of at least 2 persons, Imam and Muktadi. Muktadi stands at right of Imam just few inches behind. For 3 persons, Imam stands in front.
2. Five meeting of Muslims at Masjid creates unity and love for each other.

3. Salat of a sinful person becomes more acceptable by joining in Jamat with other pious persons.
4. It is not obligatory for women, children, sick, very old persons, and blind to attend in jamat.

Excuse from Attending Jamat

1. Heavy rain.
2. Dirty and muddy road.
3. Cold weather.
4. Stormy night.
5. Musafir with short time to catch train, plain, ship.
6. Need to go Toilet.
7. Hungry and food is being served.

Manners in Salat

1. Muqtadis should attend close to each other (no space in between) and in straight line.
2. Children should stand in back row. It is Makruh to include children in men's row.
3. If Imam's Salat is void, muqtadi's Salat is also void and must be repeated.

Who should be Iman?

1. One who knows Masail of Salat well provided he is not an open sinner.
2. Who can recite Qur'an well.
3. Who is pious.
4. Oldest person.
5. Good mannered and kind.

If there is a fixed Iman in a Masjid, then he will still deserve the honor to be the Imam. It is Makruh to make Imam a fasiq, an ignorant, one who is involved in bidat, one who is not careful in observing the rules of Shariat.

Who can NOT be Imam?

1. Insane.
2. Drunk.
3. Kefir / disbeliever.
4. Mushrik / idle worshipper.
5. Not baligh / mature.
6. Women.

Masbooq

If a person joins Salat with Iman as late as in Ruku, he is regarded as completed that rakat. If he joins after Ruku, he will not get that rakat. Such a person is called **Masbooq**.

1. A person missed any rakat, joins the Salat, he should continue with Iman to the end. When Iman turns second Salam, Masbooq should stand up and complete missed rakats.
2. If Masbooq misses one rakat, he should stand up, read Sura Fateha + one Sura and complete Salat.
3. If Masbooq misses 2 rakats in Fajr, Zuhr, Asr or Isa, he should complete both rakats with Sura Fateha + one Sura in both rakats.
4. If Masbooq misses 2 rakats in Maghrib, complete first rakat, make Qaida and Tasahud, stand up for second rakat, recite Fateha + one Sura, complete Salat.
5. If 3 rakats are missed in Zuhr, Asr, Isa, Masbooq should stand up, read Fateha + Sura in first rakat, make Ruku and sejda. Before standing for second rakat, make Qaida, read Tasahud, and stand up for second rakat. In second rakat, recite Fateha + Sura, complete second rakat and without sitting for Tasahud stand up for 3rd rakat. In 3rd rakat only Fateha is required.
6. If a person misses all rakats, he should repeat whole Salat after Iman says second Salam except he should not raise hands to say allahu akbar.
7. If a person join Jamat in Ruku, it is Fard to stand and recite Takbir Tahrima first, pause for a moment (Salat in invalid without pause) and then join in Ruku.
8. One should not join Salat as soon as Iman recites first salam.

Qaza Salat

1. Allah likes it very much when Salat is performed on time.
2. Fard and wajib Salat performed after time expired is called **Qaza**. If Asr is performed at Maghrib time, it will be Qaza.
3. To delay any Fard, wajib or Sunnate Muakkada Salat intentionally and make qaza is very sinful.
4. It is compulsory for every Muslim to perform missed number of Fard and wajib Salat since he started puberty / baligh.
5. If time remaining for regular Salat is short, regular Salat should be performed first, qaza Salat later.

6. Qaza Salat should be performed in order if less than 6 Salats are missed. If more than 5 Salats are missed, it is not necessary to pray in order.

Niyat / Intention for Qaza Salat

1. Make niyat for particular Salat for particular day.
2. If one does not remember how many Salats missed, he should make niyat of first Salat (Fajr, Zuhr etc), second Salat (Fajr, Zuhr etc)............and so on until he feels satisfied that all of his missed Salats are performed.

Musafir / Traveler's Salat

1. If a person intends to travel 48 miles or more, he is a **Musafir**.
2. If he travels 48 miles or more and intends to stay at one destination for less than 15 days, he is a Musafir.
3. If Musafir intends to stay 15 days or more, he will be Musafir during travel only. Once he reaches destination, he is not a Musafir.
4. Musafir should make qasar Salat for Zuhr, Asr, Isa i.e. perform 2 rakats of Fard instead of 4 rakats. There is no qasar for Maghrib, Witr, Sunnat or Nafl Salats.
5. If Musafir performs Salat behind a local Iman (not a Musafir), he should perform 4 rakats in Zuhr, Asr, and Isa.
6. If Imam is Musafir, he prays 2 rakats, completes his Salat and asks local Muktadi to complete their remaining rakats. The Muktadi should stand up and complete remaining 2 rakats without reciting Fateha or any Suras.

Salat for Sick: Salat is allowed in sitting position when:
1. Sick person has no strength to stand.
2. Standing causes great pain, or increase illness.
3. Can stand but cannot do Ruku or sejda.
4. If Ruku or sejda can not be performed, then they must be made by gestures i.e., bowing head slightly for Ruku and more for sejda.
5. If Salat can not be performed by sitting, it can be performed by lying.
   Lie on back with legs towards qibla. Legs should not be stretched and knees should be raised. Head should rest at a high level with pillow under it.

6. One may lie down on the right side (preferred) or left side with head towards qibla.

7. If a person faints for less than full day and night, he must perform missed Salats. If the faint duration is more than full day and night, he does not need to perform missed Salats. He is exempted and there is no qaza necessary.

8. If the patient has no strength even to move head for gesture, he should not perform Salat. If the condition continues for more than a day and night, he is not required to do qaza for missed Salats.

9. If one gains strength to move head for gesture within a day or night or for a period less than that, qaza can be performed for 5 or less Salats.

10. Tayamum is permitted if use of water will be injurious to health. He can be assisted if needed.

11. If a sick person can not move and his bed is impure, Salat is OK on the same bed.

12. If a person can not use water due to paralysis, he should use toilet paper or dry clay to clean. If he can not use anything, he can perform Salat without Istenja.

13. A person can pray lying down if he can not move head due to eye surgery.

Nafl / Optional Salats

Tahiyatul Wudu: 2 rakats of Salat offered whenever Wudu is performed.

Tahiyatul Masjid: 2 rakats of Salat may be performed after entering the Masjid before sitting.

Ishraq: After Fajr Salat, one should remain sitting on floor till sunrise with zikr, Durud, du'a etc without worldly talks or business. After sunrise, offer 2 or 4 rakats of Salat as Iraq. Its reward is equal to the reward of an accepted Hajj and Omrah.

Chast: When sun is sufficiently high and hot, 2 or 4 rakats are offered as Chast. It has very great rewards.

Awabin: After Fard and sunnat of Maghrib Salat, 6 to 12 rakats (2 rakats at a time) are offered as Awabin.

Tahajjud: Offered 4 to 12 rakats (2 rakats at a time) after mid night till Subeh Sadek. It is of great merit and virtue. If one is not sure to get up after mid night, he may offer after Isa Salat but will not get maximum rewards.

Taubah Salat: If a sin is committed, perform 2 rakats, recite Durud upon Nabi ﷺ, be ashamed and regret over the sin and seek Allah's pardon by firm pledging not to repeat the sin again. Insallah, Allah will forgive the sin.

Salat Tasbih: Rasul ﷺ said to his uncle Abbas ؓ: O my uncle! I want to make a special gift to you, so that if you act upon it, Allah will forgive all your sins, whether old or new, intentional or unintentional, minor or major, open or secret. That action is to offer 4 rakats of Nafl Salat, and during each rakat, after Sura Fateha and one Sura, recite:
Subhanallahe walhumdu lillahi wala ilaha illallahu wallahu akbar

سُبْحَانَ اللهِ وَالْحَمْدُ لِلّهِ وَلَاإِلهَ إِلاَّ اللهُ وَاللهُ أَكْبَرُ

15 times while standing, 10 times in Ruku, 10 times when rise from Ruku, 10 times in first sejda, 10 times in second sejda, 10 times when sit after second sejda. Total in each rakat is 75 times. If possible, pray this Salat once everyday, or every Friday, or once in a month, or once in a year, or **at least** once in lifetime.

Salat Istekhara: When anyone wishes to sought guidance from Allah on any important decision such as marriage, travel etc, Salat Istekhara is performed. Insallah, Allah will put good in that act. Perform 2 rakats Nafl Salat. Praise Allah by saying *alhamdulillah*: اَلْحَمْدُ لِلَّهِ

recite Durud upon Muhammad ﷺ

اَللَّهُمَّ صَلِّ عَلَى سَيِّدِنَا مُحَمَّدٍ وَعَلَى ال سيِّدِنَا مُحَمَّدٍ وَبَّارِكْ وَسَلِّمْ

Allahumma salleala sayedena Muhammdiu walaale sayedena muhammad wabarik wasallim and recite the du'a of Istekhara, think of the reason and work, sleep on a clean bed with Wudu facing Qibla.

Du'a of Istekhara

اَللَّهُمَّ إِنِّى أَسْتَخِيرُكَ بِعِلْمِكَ وَأَسْتَقْدِرُكَ بِقُدْرَتِكَ وَأَسْأَلُكَ مِنْ فَضْلِكَ الْعَظِيْمِ فَإِنَّكَ
تَقْدِرُ وَلاَ أَقْدِرُ وَتَعْلَمُ وَلاَ أَعْلَمُ وَأَنْتَ عَلاَمَ الْغُيُوْبِ اللَّهُمَّ إِنْ كُنْتَ تَعْلَمُ أَنَّ هَذَا
الْأَمْرَ خَيْرٌ لِى فِىْ دِيْنِى وَمَعَاشِى وَعَاقِبَةِ أَمْرِى فَاقْدُرْهُ لِىْ وَيَسِّرْهُ لِىْ ثُمَّ بَارِكْ لِىْ
فِيْهِ وَإِنْ كُنْتَ تَعْلَمُ أَنَّ هَذَا الْأَمْرَ شَرٌّلِى فِىْ دِيْنِى وَمَعَاشِى وَعَاقِبَةِ أَمْرِى فَاصْرِفْهُ
عَنِّى وَاصْرِفْنِى عَنْهُ وَاقْدُرْلِىَ الْخَيْرَ حَيْثُ كَانَ ثُمَّ أَرْضِنِى بِهِ

Allahumma inni astakheruka beilmeka wastakhderuka bequdrateka wasaluka minfadleka azim fainnaka taqdiru wala aqdiru wataalamu wala aalamu wanta allamul guyube allahumma inkunta taalamu anna hazal amra khairulli fiddini wamaashi waaqibati amri faqdirhu li wayassirhuli summa barikli fihe wainkunta taalamu anna haazal amra sharruli fiddini wamaashi waqibati amri fusrifhu anni wasrifuni anhu waakdiru lil khaira haisu kana summa ardinibihi.

(O Allah, I ask of You the good through Your knowledge and I ask You to grant me ability through Your power and beg Your Favor out of Your infinite bounty. For surely, You have power and I have none. You know all and I know not. You are The Knower of all that is hidden. O Allah, if, in Your knowledge, this matter of good for my faith, my livelihood and the consequences of my affairs in the world and the hereafter then ordain it for me and make it easy for me and bless me therein. But if, in Your knowledge, this matter be bad for my faith, my livelihood and the consequences of my affairs in the world or the hereafter then turn it away from me and turn me away from there and ordain for me the good wherever it be and cause me to be pleased therewith).

Act on the decision comes in the heart after wake up. This process can be continued up to 7 days if no decision is reached.
There is no Istekhara on Fard duty such as Salat, Hajj, Zakat etc.

Chapter - 4: Juma + Eid + Janaza Salat / Prayer

Juma / Friday Salat

1. Allah says in Qur'an: O you who believe! When call is made for Salat on Friday, hasten to the remembrance of Allah and leave off business. That is better for you if you know. When the Salat is completed, disperse through the land and seek Allah's grace and remember Allah often that you may be successful (Al-Jumah:9).
2. Juma Salat is **Fard** on Friday in place of Zuhr Salat. There is no Zuhr Fard Salat on Friday. It is Fard for all except minor children, slaves, mad, sick, blind, Musafir, women and those with valid excuse such as fear of enemy, heavy rain. They should perform Zuhr Salat instead.
3. Juma Salat has 14 Rakats. See table for requirements.

Conditions for Juma Salat

1. It should be in a city, big village, town, not in a small village.
2. It should be performed at Zuhr time.
3. Khutba should be delivered before Salat.
4. Salat should be with Jamat. It is compulsory to have at least 3 besides imam to make Salat valid.
5. Permission to all to attend.

Method of Khutba Delivery

1. Before Juma Salat, Imam should sit on mimbar / raised platform and Moazzin should call azan in presence of Imam. Iman should stand up and deliver Khutba facing congregation. It is makrooh tahreme to deliver Khutba in any language besides Arabic.
2. After first Khutba, Imam sits down for a while and then stands up again for second Khutba. Then Imam steps down and stand in front of mehrab / arch. The Moazzin calls the Iqamat and those present should stand up, form line shoulder to shoulder, offer Salat with Imam.

Forbidden During Khutba

It is wajib / compulsory to listen to the Khutba. It is part of Juma Salat. If Khutba has already started when someone arrives, he should immediately sit and listen to Khutba. Talking, offer sunnat and Nafl Salats, eating, drinking, reply to any talk, recite Qur'an etc are not permitted.

Eid Salat (Fitr and Azha)

Mustahab and Sunnat on Eid days
1. Take bath and meswak.
2. Use best clothes and itr / fragrance.
3. Eat dates or any sweet before Eidul Fitr Salat.
4. Give **Sadqatul Fitr** before Eidul Fitr Salat.
5. Go by foot, go by one route and return by another route.
6. Do not perform Nafl at home or at Eid place before and after Eid Salat.
7. Say Takbir with low voice while going for Eidul Fitr Salat.

اَللّٰهُ اَكْبَرُ اَللّٰهُ اَكْبَرُ لَاإِلٰهَ إِلاَّ اللّٰهُ وَاللّٰهُ اَكْبَرُ اَللّٰهُ اَكْبَرُ وَلِلّٰهِ الْحَمْدُ

Allahu akbar allahu akbar lailaha illallahu aallahu akbar allahu akbar walillahel hamd. (Allah is great Allah is great There is no deity besides Allah and Allah is great and all praise belongs to Him alone).
8. Say Takbir little loud while going for Eidul Adha Salat.
9. There is no azan or Iqamat in Eid Salat.
10. There are 2 rakats in each Eid Salat with 6 extra Takbirs.
11. Khutba is not Fard for Eid, Khutba after Salat is sunnat.
12. Perform Eid Salat at a place fixed for Eid.
13. Eat meat of sacrificed animal after Eidul Adha Salat.

How to perform Eid Salat?
1. Make niyat: I am performing 2 rakats of Eidul Fitr or Eidul Azha Wajib with six (6) extra Takbirs behind Imam, *allahu akbar.*
2. Fold hands after *Takbire Tahrima* and read Sana.
3. Raise hands up to ears, bring down while saying *allahu akbar*
4. Do the same 2nd time.
5. 3rd time raise hands up to ears and say *allahu akbar,* hold them below navel.
6. Imam reads tasbih, Fateha, another Sura and then go to Ruku.
7. When stand up for second rakat, Imam recites qirat, say *allahu akbar*, raise hands up to ears and let them down.
8. Again repeat second, 3rd, 4th time, go to Ruku.........and complete Salat.
9. Imam stands up, deliver Khutba, all should sit silently and hear Khutba.
10. There are 2 khutbas for each Eid. Imam sits in between and it is Masnoon.
11. It is wajib / compulsory to listen Khutba.

Janaza / Funeral

1. A person is about to die is called **Muhtadar**. It is sunnat to let him lie on right side facing Qibla. It is OK to lie on back and feet towards Qibla with face slightly raised. Don't move if movement causes discomfort.
2. It is OK to use fragrance. Any unclean person should not be there.
3. Muhtadar should recite Sura Yasin or someone recites any part of Qur'an. Remind the dying person of 2 sahadats (1st and 2nd Kalima).
4. Before death, he breathes frequently, knees become weak, nose bents and temperature falls. Muhtadar must not be asked or ordered to read Kalima but help to recall it by reciting loudly in front of him. Once Muhtadar recites Kalema, all should remain silent. Avoid any worldly discussion.
5. After Muhtadar passes away, mouth and eyes should be closed, feet be tied together, body covered with a clean sheet. Recite du'a:

inna lillahe wainna ilaihe razeun اِنَّا لِلّٰهِ وَاِنَّا اِلَيْهِ رَاجِعُوْنَ

(To Allah do we belong, and to Him shall we return).
6. It is Makruh to recite Qur'an near a dead person between death and Gusl.

Actions after Death
1. Obtain doctor's certificate, if required.
2. Obtain burial order, if required.
3. Obtain death certificate.
4. Obtain removal order from police if required.
5. Process legal requirements if necessary.
6. Inform relatives and friends and time of Janaza.
7. Prepare grave.
8. Perform Gusl.
9. Put kafan / grave clothes.
10. Arrange transportation for cemetery if necessary.

Kafan Requirements
Kafan is grave clothes of the dead and it is preferred to be white. It does not have to be good quality. It is OK to prepare one's Kafan earlier to avoid last minute rush. Following types of clothes are for kafan:

1. Sheet: 4 m x 140 cm, 150 cm, 180 cm wide depending on the size of body (1.75 m for Izar and 2.25 m for lifafa) or
2. Calico: 8 m x 90 cm wide (3.5 m for Izar and 4.5 m for lifafa).
3. These are cut in half and sewn together.
4. Calico: 1.8 m, 90 cm wide for qames.
5. Any other material 2.5 m x 115 cm
6. 60 grams of camphor.
7. One small bottle of itr / fragrance.

Kafan for Male: Masnoon Kafan is to have Izar, Qames and Lifafa. Izar is a sheet from head to feet, Qames is a long sheet that is folded in half and an opening cut to put on as shirt but without pockets, sleeves or seams. Lifafa is a sheet from above head to below feet. Izar and lifafa are sufficient but it is sunnat to use 3 pieces. It is makrooh to use less than 2 without a valid reason.

Kafan for Female: Masnoon kafan is to have Izar, kimar, qames, lifafa and a piece of material to hold the breasts. Kimar is the veil. Material piece should run from breasts to the thighs. Izar, lifafa and kimar are sufficient but it is sunnat to use 5. It is makrooh to use less than three except when not available. Husband is responsible to pay her burial expenses. Kafan should not be scented with itr.

Grave Requirements
1. Unbaked bricks, bamboo, timber where ground is soft.
2. Sufficient spades.
3. Depth of grave according to height of deceased.
4. It is Makruh to dig and prepare one's own grave during one's lifetime.

2 Types of Grave
1. **Lahad:** Regular rectangular grave with Qibla side little inclined for a recess to place the body. Unbaked bricks, bamboo, timber are used to close the recess.
2. **Shiq:** When soft ground does not allow Lahad type grave, Shiq type grave is prepared with no recess but with a shallow trench at the bottom center to place the body in the trench. Timer, bamboo may be used to cover but not fabrics, blankets.

Janaza Gusl Requirements

1. Clean with luke warm water.
2. A bench or platform.
3. Two large buckets of warm water.
4. Pouring mugs, Soap, 250 gm cotton wool.
5. 2 sheets- one to cover during Gusl and one to cover before and after Gusl.
6. Scissor to remove dead's clothes.
7. Towel for drying.

Who can Perform Janaza Gusl?

1. Father, son or brother should perform for male. Mother, daughter, sister should perform for female. If none of these persons are present then near relative or pious person can perform duty (male for male, female for female). The person performing the Gusl must be clean and in Wudu. It is Makruh for women with menstruation or nifas (period after child birth) to perform Gusl.
2. For male, if no body is available then no women besides his wife can perform Gusl.
3. For women, if no ladies are available then, still husband can not perform Gusl for his wife.

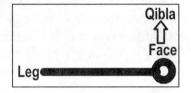

4. In both cases Tayamum can be performed instead of Gusl.
5. Any adult, male or female can perform Gusl to a child before reached puberty, if same sex person is not available.

Gusl procedure

1. It is OK to place body with legs facing Qibla or face towards Qibla.
2. No hair or nail cut is allowed. All rings, jewelry should be removed. Denture should be removed.
3. Put body on platform, cover satr.
4. Stomach should gently be massaged; both Istenja places should be washed without looking.
5. Nostrils, ears, mouth be closed with cotton to stop water to enter.
6. Wudu is performed except gargle and water into nostrils.

7. If the dead is in janabat, haiz / menstruation, nifas (Gusl is wajib), then mouth need to be gargled and nostrils be made wet with cotton wool.
8. After Wudu, head and beard should be washed with soap.
9. Body should be tilted on one side to wash right side 3 times with soap from head to toe. Similarly for left side.
10. Body is lifted to a sitting position, stomach is massaged with downward stroke, and whatever comes out should be washed. Wudu and Gusl need not be repeated.
11. Use cotton to remove water from mouth, ears, and nose.
12. When Gusl is complete, body is wiped. Satr must be covered.
13. Body should be covered with kafan sheets.

Use of Kafan / Male

1. Put lifafa on floor, Izar on top, then portion of qames under body. Top cover is placed at head side.
2. Put body on kafan, cover top body with folded portion of qames.
3. Remove sheets used for Gusl.
4. Rub fragrance on head and beard.
5. Fold left flap and then right flap of Izar over qames.
6. Fold lifafa same manner.
7. Fasten ends of lifafa at head side, feet and middle with strips of cloth.

Use of Kafan / Female

1. Spread lifafa on ground, then material, then Izar, then qames as for male. Material must be placed between Izar and qames or over lifafa.
2. Put body on kafan, cover body top up to cuffs with portion of qames.
3. Remove sheets used for Gusl.
4. Do not use itr, surma or make-up.
5. Hair is divided into 2 parts and put onto right and left breast over qames.
6. Cover head and hair.
7. Fold Izar, left flap first, then right over qames.
8. Close breast cover.
9. Close lifafa, left flaps first, then right.
10. Fasten ends of lifafa at head, feet and around middle with strips of cloth, complete kafan.

Prohibited in Kafan
1. Any charter or du'a in kafan.
2. Write Kalima or du'a on kafan or on chest.

After Kafan
1. It is OK for Mahrom women such as wife, mother, grand mother, sisters, aunts, grand daughters to see face of dead male.
2. It is OK for Mahrom males such as husband, father, grand father, brothers, uncles, sons, grand sons to see face of dead female.
3. In both cases, face should not be kept open.
4. It is OK to read Qur'an after Gusl.
5. After kafan, Salatul Janaza should be performed quickly and be buried quickly to nearby cemetery. To transport body to long distances, or delay Janaza for large crowd is Makruh.

Carry Dead
1. For adult, 4 men should carry on shoulder; for infant, child, individual can carry by hands.
2. Lift with Bismillah, carry forward. It is Mustahab for each bearer to carry 40 steps
3. Attending persons should not sit until body is lowered to grounds except sick or excused.
4. It is Masnoon to carry hastily but not shaking the body.
5. It is Mustahab to follow body and not go ahead.
6. It is Makruh for people to recite du'a or Qur'an loudly, can read Kalema softly, no worldly discussion, no joke or laugh.

Place and Time of Janaza
1. It should not be performed in Masjid but any open space or in a building. If performed in graveyard, no grave should be in front of jamat or use obstruction.
2. Besides the forbidden times (sunrise, Zawal, sunset), any other times can be used for Janaza Salat including after Asr Salat.

Janaza Salat / Prayer

- Janaza is **Farde Kifaya** on all Muslims i.e., if some Muslims take care of Janaza, responsibility is over otherwise every Muslim is responsible.
- It consists of 4 Takbirs, Sana, Durud, Masnoon du'a for dead and 2 salams. Imam and everybody say all these silently. Imam calls out Takbirs and Salams loudly.

2 Fard in Janaza
1. To stand and perform Salat,
2. To recite all 4 Takbirs.

Janaza procedure
1. Body is placed with head on right side of Iman facing Qibla.
2. Imam stands in line with the chest of the dead during Salat.
3. It is Mustahab to make odd number of rows. Rows should be close to each other as there is no sejda to make.
4. When rows are straightened, Niyat is made: *I am performing Janaza for Allah behind this Imam.* After Niyat, raise hands up to ears, Imam says *allahu akbar* loudly, others quietly. Then fold hands below navel like daily Salat. Recite Sana.
5. Iman recites Takbir loudly, others quietly for 2nd time. Hands should not be raised any more. *Durude Ibrahim* should be recited.
6. Takbir is made 3rd time. Recite following du'a for **adult male or female**:

اَللَّهُمَّ اغْفِرْ لِحَيِّنَا وَمَيِّتِنَا وَشَاهِدِنَا وَغَائِبِنَا وَصَغِيْرِنَا وكَبِيْرِنَا وَذَكَرْنَ وَأُنْثَانَا اَللَّهُمَّ مَنْ أَحْيَيْتَهُ مِنَّا فَأَحْيِهِ عَلَى الإِسْلاَمِ وَمَنْ تَوَفَّيْتَهُ مِنَّا فَتَوَفَّهُ عَلَى الإِيْمَانِ

Allahumughfirli hyyena wamyyetena washahedena waghaebena wasaghirena wakabirena wazakarena waunsana. allahumma mun ahyytahu minna faahyihi alal islame waman tawaffytahu minna fatawaffahu alal imaan. (O Allah! Forgive those of us that are dead, those of us that present, and those of us who are absent, those of us that are young, and those of us that are adults; our males and our females. O Allah! Whomsoever of us You keep alive, let him live as a follower of Islam and whomsoever You cause to die, let him die as a believer.

7. Make following du'a for **minor**

اَللَّهُمَّ اجْعَلْهُ لَنَا فَرَطًا وَّاجْعَلْهُ لَنَا اَجْرًا وَّذُخْرًا وَّاجْعَلْهُ لَنَا شَافِعًا وَّمُشَفَّعًا

Allahummazalhu lana farataw wajalhu lana azraw wazukhraw wazalha lana shafiaw wa mushaffa. (O Allah! Make him / her a source for our salvation and make him / her a source of reward and treasure for us, and make him / her an intercessor for us, and one whose intercession is accepted).

8. Imam should say 4th Takbir, recite Salam 2 times turning face first right then left. Others follow and say softly.

9. For late comers, join immediately with Tayamum (for Janaza only) if time does not allow making Wudu. Join after any Takbir by Imam. Complete all missed Takbirs after Imam finishes without any du'a.

Burial Process

1. Bury dead as soon as possible after Janaza Salat. Place head on right side of grave facing Qibla. Close relatives (of female body) should help lower the body. Husband should not enter grave to bury his wife.

2. It is Mustahab to hold a sheet over the grave while lowering and burying a female and to recite this du'a while the body is being lowered.

   Bismillahe Wala Millate Rasulullah. بِسْمِ اللهِ وَعَلَى مِلَّةِ رَسُوْلِ اللهِ
   (In the name of Allah and on the creed, religion and faith of Rasulullah).

3. After the body is placed into the recess of the grave, it is Masnoon to turn body on right side to face Qibla. The cloth strip at head side, chest and leg side should be untied.

4. The recess should be covered with unbaked bricks, bamboo or timber.

How to Fill Grave and Shape

1. It is Mustahab to start filling recess from the leg side for males, from head side for females. All the remaining areas should be filled with mud or grass and not any fabric or blanket.

2. Everyone present should fill with at least 3 handful of soil.

3. It is *Makruh* to add more soil than what was dug out.

During **First** fill, recite…	During **Second** fill, recite…	During **Third** fill, recite…
مِنْهَا خَلَقْنَكُمْ	وَفِيْهَا نُعِيْدُكُمْ	وَمِنْهَا نُخْرِجُكُمْ تَارَةً أُخْرى
Minha khalaknakum (From the (earth) did We create you)	*Wafiha nuidukum* (and into it shall We return you)	*Waminha nukhrizukum taratun ukhra* (and from it shall We bring you once again)

4. The grave shape should be like hump of a camel with a height of 10-12 inches. It should not be like square or any other shape. All

types of building or enclosure on or around grave are not permissible.

5. It is Mustahab to recite Qur'an / du'a for deceased after it is filled.
6. After the burial, recite the first Ruku of Sura Baqara at the headside and the last Ruku of Sura Baqara at the leg side.

Visit Graveyard

1. Visit any day preferably Friday.
2. Recite Qur'an / du'a as much as possible for dead's forgiveness.
3. Recite Sura Ikhlas 11 times, reciting Sura Yasin eases punishment.
4. Do not place wreaths, flowers, candle etc.

Iddat Period

1. Iddat is 4 months and 10 days of waiting period after one's husband dies. During this period, she should stay at the house where she lived with her husband. If she is pregnant at the time of her husband's death, her Iddat will be until the birth of the child. If she is not at home when her husband dies, she should return as soon as possible and spend the Iddat period at home. During Iddat period, she should abstain from fancy cloths, makeup or jewelry.
2. Trustee of the dead should pay all debts as soon as possible. *Isale Sawab* can be made by feeding poor, give sadqa, make istegfar for the dead. No specific day such as 3rd, 7th, 11th 14th should be used. No specific color of cloth is defined. For stillborn, baby of miscarriage, body is wrapped and buried without Janaza. For one Muslim parent child and suicide dead person, Janaza should be performed. Women do not follow Janaza nor visit graveyard.

Chapter – 5: Saum / Fasting

Fasting means to stay away from eating, drinking, and sex from early dawn to sunset. Ramadan fasting is **Fard** upon every Muslim, male and female who is sane and mature. There is lot of reward of fasting and severe punishment for not fasting. Fasting has many physical, moral or social benefits.

Virtues of Fasting: Muhammad ﷺ says:
1. When Ramadan comes, doors of heaven are opened, hells are closed, and devils are chained.
2. The fragrance of the mouth of a fasting person is more pleasant to Allah than smell of musk.
3. One door named Rayyan of heaven is reserved for those who fast.
4. Whoever breaks fast one day in Ramadan without excuse, his whole life fasting can not compensate it. Eat sehri before dawn, because it has blessing.
5. Whoever fasts during Ramadan with hope for reward, all his sins will be forgiven.
6. Fasting experiences kindness by rich towards poor.

Type of Fasting
1. **Farde Muaiyan** - Fasting for the whole month of Ramadan.
2. **Frade Gair Muaiyan** - Fasting to keep qaza of missed days of Ramadan with or without reason.
3. **Wajib Muaiyan** - Keep fasting on a specific day or date upon fulfillment of some wish or desire.
4. **Wajib Gair Muaiyan** - Pledge to keep fast without fixing any day or date upon fulfillment of wish. Fast for breaking one's oath.
5. **Sunnat** - Fasting on 9th and 10th Muharram, 9th Zil Hajj etc.
6. **Mustahab** - Fast on Monday and Thursday.
7. **Makruh** - Fast only on 9th or 10th Muharram or on Saturdays.
8. **Haram** - Fast 5 days during the year such as Eidul Fitr, Eidul Adha, 3 days after Eidul Adha.

Intention: Fast without Niyat / Intention is not valid. It is not necessary to express verbally but can be in heart. Niyat should be made before dawn.

Du'a to Start Fast:

بِصَوْمِ غَدٍ نَوَيْتُ

Besaume ghadin nawaitu
(I intend to fast
tomorrow)

Du'a to Break Fast:

اَللّٰهُمَّ لَكَ صُمْتُ وَبِكَ اٰمَنْتُ وَعَلٰى رِزْقِكَ اَفْطَرْتُ

Allahumma laka sumtu wabeka amuntu waala rizqeka afturtu.
(O Allah, for Your sake I have fasted, and with what You provided, I break my fast)

Mustahab of Fasting

1. Sehri / meal before dawn.
2. Delay sehri till just before dawn.
3. Break fast immediately after sunset.
4. Break with dry or fresh dates if available or water.
5. Make niyat at night.

6 Sunnats of Fasting

1. Eat sehri.
2. Break fast immediately after sunset.
3. Read Tarawih at night.
4. Feed poor and hungry.
5. Increase reading Qur'an.
6. Make I'tikaf at Masjid during last 10 days of Ramadan.

Don't Do during Fasting

1. Speak without reason.
2. Rude, Irritate people.
3. Tell lies, swear.
4. Backbite.
5. Argue or fight.
6. Be boastful and arrogant.
7. Eat doubtful food at iftar.
8. Look at undesirable things.
9. Listen to bad speech.
10. Gossip, commit any sin.

Makruh during Fasting: (not desirable)

1. Chew gum, rubber, plastic items.
2. Taste any food or drink and spit it out. For a hot-tempered husband, wife can taste food provided it does not go down the throat.
3. Collect one's saliva in mouth and swallow it to quench thirst.
4. Delay Fard bath knowingly until after dawn.

5. Use of toothpaste or powder to clean teeth. Meswak is OK.
6. Complain of hunger and thirst.
7. Too much water to nostrils during nose cleaning.
8. Gargle more than necessary.
9. Quarrel, argue, use filthy or indecent words.
10. Backbite, tell lie and swear etc.

Fasting Breakers
2 kinds of Fasting Breakers
1. Qaza (broken intentionally before)
2. Need Qaza and compulsory Kaffara (60 days fasting continuously or feed 60 poor people, or feed one poor for 60 days).

Qaza Fasting under Following Conditions
1. Put anything in mouth by force.
2. Water down the throat during gargle.
3. Vomit mouthful intentionally.
4. Swallow pebble, paper or any item that is not food or medicine.
5. Swallow something edible, equal to or bigger than a grain of gram stuck between teeth intentionally.
6. Put oil in ear.
7. Inhale snuff into the nostrils.
8. Swallow blood from gums.
9. Eat / drink by mistake, then eat / drink thinking fast is broken.
10. Eat and drink after *Subeh Sadeq* or break fast before sunset due to cloudy sky or faulty watch and then realize one's fault.
11. Any fast other than Ramadan, whether broken intentionally or with valid reason, needs Qaza only.

Reasons for Qaza with Kaffara / Penalty
Eat, drink, smoke, and break fast without valid reason.
Apply surma in eye or rub oil on head and think fast is broken, then start eating or drinking.
Drink any medicine intentionally, however injection is permitted.

Things DON'T Break Fasting
1. Eat or drink by mistake.
2. Mosquito, fly or any object go through throat by mistake.
3. Water enters ears.
4. Dust or dirt through throat.
5. Swallow one's saliva.
6. Take injection.

7. Apply surma in eyes.
8. Take bath.
9. Rub oil on body or hair.
10. Vomit unintentionally.
11. Apply perfume, but can't inhale smoke or cigarette.
12. Brush teeth without paste.
13. Dream, which makes Gusl necessary, does not break fast.

Exempt from Ramadhan Fasting

1. Sick person when health affected by fasting. After recovery, fast day for day.
2. A traveler beyond 48 miles and not intended for more than 14 days.
3. If afraid of death due to hunger or thirst.
4. It is compulsory to make qaza of a Nafl fast if broken.

Compensation / Fidya of Fasting

1. If old without enough strength or sick can not fast in Ramadan, then Fidya for a fast can be given as: 3.5 lbs of wheat or 7 lbs of barley or equivalent cash to poor. If old or sick person recovers after Ramadan, he must fast for missed days.
2. No one can fast for another person even sick or old.

I'tikaf: I'tikaf means to enter and reside at Masjid.

3 types of I'tikaf

1. **Wajib** - pledged to make I'tikaf on a fixed day for Allah upon fulfillment of wish / desire. Minimum time: one day and night with a fast.
2. **Sunnat** - reside last 10 nights and days of Ramadan. It is Sunnate Muakkada. If someone does, entire community is relieved otherwise it becomes obligatory for everyone.
3. **Mustahab** - can be for any amount of time or few minutes.

Conditions of I'tikaf

1. Muslim, 2. Not mad, 3. Free from taharat, 4. Intention.

Permitted During I'tikaf

1. Eat, 2. Sleep, 3. Discuss Deen, 4. Leave Masjid for wajib Gusl, 5. Wudu, 6. Toilet.

Activities During I'tikaf

1. Ibadat, 2. Recite Qur'an, 3. Nafl Salat and zikr, 4. Durud sarif and Istegfar, 5. Learn / teach Deen.

I'tikaf for women: should be at her home or any suitable place.

Niyat of I'tikaf

نَوَيْتُ الْاِعْتِكَافَ لِلّهِ عَزَّ وَجَلَّ مَادُمْتُ فِى الْمَسْجِدِ

Nawaitul itekafa lillahe azza wajalla madumtu fil masjede
(I intend making I'tikaf for Allah till I remain in Masjid).

Tarawih Salat

1. It is Sunnate Muakkada for men or women.
2. It is Sunnate Kifaya for men in jamat.
3. It is OK to perform at home but preferred at Masjid.
4. Tarawih Salat time is from Isha to *Subeh Sadeq*. It can be performed before or after Witr Salat.
5. If Imam starts Witr after Tarawih, join Salat for Witr and complete Tarawih later.
6. 20 rakats with 10 Salams are Masnoon with 2 rakats each time. After each 4 rakats, it is Mustahab to sit a while.

Tarawih Du'a

سُبْحَانَ ذِىْ الْمُلْكِ وَالْمَلَكُوْتِ سُبْحَانَ ذِى الْعِزَّةِ وَالْعَظْمَةِ وَالْهَيْبَةِ وَالْقُدْرَةِ وَالْكِبْرِيَا
وَالْجَبَرُوْتِ سُبْحَانَ الْمَلِكِ الْحَىِّ الَّذِى لَايَنَامُ وَلَايَمُوْتُ سُبُّوْحٌ قُدُّوْسٌ رَبُّنَا وَرَبُّ
الْمَلَئِكَةُ وَالرُّوْحِ اللّهُمَّ اَجِرْنَا مِنَ النَّارِ يَامُجِيْرُ يَامُجِيْرُ يَامُجِيْر

Subhanazil mulke walmalakute subhanazil ezzate walazmate walhybate walqudrate walkibriyae waljabarute. subhanal malikil hyallazi laya namu wala-yamutu subbuhun kuddusun rabbuna warabbul malaekati warruhe. allahumma ajirna minun nare yamujiru yamujiru yamujiru.

(Glorified is the Owner of the sovereignty (of the earth and the heavens). Glorified is the Owner of honor and greatness, and dignity and omnipotence and might. Glorified is the Living Sovereign who neither sleeps nor dies. Highly hallowed and sacred is He, our Lord and the Lord of the angels and the spirits. O lord! Save us from Hell. O Savior! O Savoir! O Savoir).

7. One may remain silent, recite Qur'an or tasbih or pray Nafl Salat during rest period.
8. It is Makruh to perform Tarawih sitting if one can stand.
9. It is Makruh to wait to join Iman at Ruku if one can join earlier.
10. If one misses Fard, then he should perform Fard alone and then join Tarawih.

Chapter – 6: Zakat

Zakat is one of the 5 pillars of Islam. It means to increase. It means to purify one's wealth by distributing 2.5% to poor or needy. It is not a tax but a compulsory duty from Allah to pay to needy.

Virtues of Zakat

1. Allah says in Qur'an: Allah ﷻ destroys wealth obtained from interest and will give increase for deed of charity. *(Baqara: 276).*
2. The nation that does not give Zakat, Allah will bring draught.
3. The person on whom Allah bestowed wealth and he does not give Zakat, on the day of kiamat, his wealth will be turned into a venomous bald serpent which will wind around his neck and bite his jaws and say "I am your wealth" *(Bukhari).*

Benefits of Zakat

1. Please Allah.
2. Increase wealth.
3. Barakat in wealth.
4. Protect from loss.
5. Safe from calamities.
6. Receive Allah's blessings and forgiveness.
7. Protect from wrath of Allah.
8. Provide shelter on day of judgment.
9. Security from 70 misfortunes.
10. Save from hellfire.
11. Saves from moral ill of love and greed for wealth.
12. Zakat helps poor, widow, orphans, disabled, and destitute in the society.

Punishment for NOT giving Zakat

Allah says in Qur'an: There are those who hoard gold and silver and do not spend it in the way of Allah, announce to them a most grievous penalty on the day of Qiyamah. Heat will be produced out of wealth in the fire of hell, they will be branded with it on their foreheads and their flanks and backs. (They will be told) This is the treasure, which you hoarded for yourselves, tastes the treasure that you had been hoarding *(At-Tauba:34).*

Whom Zakat is Fard
1. Muslim.
2. Adult.
3. Sane person.
4. Free person - not a slave.
5. Owns wealth intended for trading to value of Nisab.
6. Wealth fully owned.
7. Excess of personal needs such as cloth, furniture, utensils, car etc.
8. Wealth possessed for a complete lunar year.
9. Productive wealth from which profit or benefit can be derived such as merchandise for business, gold, silver, livestock etc. Zakat is not required on non-productive wealth.

Type of Wealth on which Zakat IS Fard
1. Gold and silver in any form with value equal to Nisab rate.
2. Gold less than 87.48 grams or silver less than 612.36 grams but combined value is equal to either gold or silver Nisab then Zakat is Fard.
3. If gold or silver is more in a mixture with other metal, then whole amount is considered as gold or silver and Zakat is Fard. If other metal is more, Zakat will not be Fard.
4. If a person has 620 grams of silver (more than Nisab) and before a whole year has elapsed, he acquires 50 grams of gold (less than Nisab), then value of gold must be added to silver and Nisab is reckoned. Two must not be reckoned separately to avoid Zakat.
5. Zakat is Fard on merchandise for business if equal to Nisab.
6. Zakat is Fard on livestock.
7. Zakat is Fard on income of properties if equal to Nisab.
8. Zakat is Fard on income from renting business.

Type of Wealth on which Zakat IS NOT Fard
1. Zakat is not Fard on any other metal besides gold and silver,
2. Zakat is not Fard on fixtures, fittings, accessories which are used to run business,
3. There is no Zakat on diamond, pearl, other precious stones for personal use. Zakat is Fard on gold or silver used in jewellery with stones. No Zakat on imitation jewelry.
4. No Zakat on house, furniture, clothes whether in use or not.
5. No Zakat if liabilities exceed or equal to assets.
6. A person has $300 but owes $200, Zakat is due on $100.

Zakat on Animals

1. Zakat is Fard on halal animals such as cow, camel if they graze on open field for greater part of year and not stall-fed.
2. Zakat on saima animals (kept for milk, breeding) is calculated on number (not value) including crossbreed. Zakat is calculated for animals kept for trade as any commercial business.
3. Zakat from each category of mixed animals will be given (if Nisab hits) from its own kind.
4. If number of each type does not hit Nisab but total does, then Zakat from greatest type should be given.
5. If both types are equal in number, any type can be used to pay.

Zakat NOT Fard on Animals

1. If animals are stall-fed for 6 months and then left to graze for rest of the year are not saima and Zakat is not required.
2. No Zakat on animals used for riding, own use or consumption.
3. No Zakat on wild animal.
4. No Zakat on horse, donkey and mule if not for trade.
5. No Zakat on heard with calves only until they reach age of breeding. If the heard has one animal that can be used for breeding, then Zakat for the entire heard must be given.
6. Zakat is not required on sheep less than 12 months old.

Nisab and Rate of Zakat

Nisab is the amount of Zakat liable from wealth if possessed for a full Islamic year. Gold – 87.48 grams, silver - 612.36 grams. Rate is 2.5%

Zakat for sheep and goats only if more than 12 years old and at least 40 in number.

40-120   = 1 animal,
121-200   = 2 animals,
201-399   = 3 animals,
400   = 4 animals.
For each additional 100, one more animal.

Zakat for Cattle and Buffaloes:

30-39 = 1 animal / 1year old,
40-59 = 1 animal / 2 year old,
60-69 = 2 animals / 1 year old.
For every 30 animals =1 animal / 1 yr old
For each 40 = 1 animal / 2 year old.

#	1 year old	2 year old
70	1	1
80		2
90	3	
100	2	1
110	1	2
120	4	or 3

Niyat / Intention of Zakat

1. Niyat is Fard when giving Zakat to needy. Zakat is invalid without niyat.
2. It is not necessary to mention to the needy as Zakat.
3. If Zakat amount is set aside and niyat is made but forget while giving Zakat, Zakat is valid.

Method Zakat Distribution

1. Zakat (2.5%) should be given as soon as possible after it is due.
2. A poor man can not be paid for work as Zakat, nor Zakat can be given for any service except an Islamic government who can pay someone as salary to collect Zakat.
3. Zakat is only valid when recipient is made owner of the Zakat amount.
4. Zakat can not be given or used for construction of Masjid, madras a, hospital, and well, bridge or any public project.
5. Poor student can be given Zakat – directly to him if proper age or to parents / guardian if not proper age. Zakat can be paid from same merchandise or cash but must be made owner.
6. Authority to deliver can be delegated to another person or organization but it must follow the laws of Zakat.
7. If an agent or organization is given Zakat for distribution but was not distributed, then burden of Fard Zakat payment still lies on the person not the agent.
8. It is best to give Zakat when due and not wait for Ramadan.

Zakat Receiver

- **Fuqara**: Who is poor and possesses more than basic needs but do not posses equal to Nisab.
- **Masakin:** Destitute and extremely needy and forced to beg for daily food.
- **Al Amilin:** Appointed by Islamic government to collect Zakat. It is not necessary that he is needy.
- **Mu Allafatul Qulub**: Recently accepted Islam and in need of basic necessities.
- **Ar Riqab:** Slave permitted to work for remuneration and was permitted by master to purchase freedom on payment for fixed amounts.

- **Al Garimin:** Person with debt and does not posses any other wealth or goods to repay what he owes. It is conditional that this debt was not created for any unislamic / sinful activity.
- **Fe Sabilillah:** One who has to carry out a Fard and unable (due to loss of wealth) to complete.
- **Ibn Us Sabil:** A traveler who needs basic necessity (during journey) to return home, through he is well to do at home.

1. It is not permissible for a person, who has Nisab wealth to accept Zakat.
2. Books of scholar or tools of tradesman are their necessities. Besides these if he does not possess nafsi, he can accept Zakat.
3. Poor and needy relatives should be given preference. You don't need to mention as Zakat.
4. Zakat can be given to poor who is striving for Deen or engaged in religious knowledge or institution (running according to Sariah) where poor or needy students are cared for.
5. Son of a rich person who does not possess Nisab amount can receive Zakat.

Who CAN'T get Zakat

1. Banu Hashim – children of Fatima *radiallahu tala anhuma*, member of Rasul ﷺ and wives.
2. Parents, grandfather, children and grandchildren, husband and wife to each other.
3. Institutions, which do not distribute to poor students but use for construction, investment or salaries, purchase books or land.
4. Non-Muslims including Nafl sadqa.
5. If recipient is not properly investigated and later found to be wealthy, Zakat need to be paid again.
6. Zakat cannot be used for kafan of dead, as he cannot own.
7. Dead person's debt can not be paid by Zakat.

Zakat on Loan: It is due on money / valuables whether it is loan or debt.

3 types of Loan

1. **Qawi (secure loan):** If cash, gold or silver received as loan or merchandise which is sold on term payment and is received after one year or two and value is Nisab, then Zakat is Fard. If loan is repaid in installments and repayment equals to 20% of Nisab, then

Zakat on this 20% is Fard. If several years have passed, then Zakat for all years is due with 20% as Nisab. If any such loan is not equal to Nisab, then Zakat is not due. But if loan and other possession equals Nisab, then Zakat on entire amount is Fard.

2. **Mutawassi (insufficient secure loan)**: If loan is not cash, gold or silver or merchandise (as in 1), but of personal nature such as clothes, household items and the value is Nisab level, it is called Mutawassi loan. Zakat for those years prior to payment is not Fard. If loan is equal to or excess of Nisab and is fully recovered after several years, if Zakat is not Fard on past years. If repayment of loan is made in installments, Zakat is Fard only repayment is equal to Nisab and retained for one year. If installment received is less than Nisab but when added to other possession, is higher than Nisab then Zakat is due on total.

3. **Daef (insecure loan)**: If money owed to one is not in lieu of cash, gold, silver, merchandise or personal property but due to outstanding inheritance, dowry, salary etc then it is called Daef loan. Zakat will be Fard when this money is received which is equal to Nisab and retained for one year. There is no Zakat on provident fund, pension fund. If funds are received then Zakat is due.

Zakat on Merchandise

1. Articles that are purchased for resale are called merchandise. Zakat is Fard if amount is equal to Nisab.
2. Zakat is Fard on stocks, goods in trade, cash in hand, outstanding cash and loan, cash in bank, savings account, fixed deposits, claims, other savings. All these must be added together, subtract creditor amount, balance is the profit which must be added to the capital for Zakat.
3. If a bad debt is recovered and it is equal / exceeds Nisab, Zakat on all past years must be given.
4. If one has different types of merchandise then total value of all goods must be used to pay Zakat.
5. If one has Nisab amount at the beginning of the year and during the year the amount decreases and by the end of the year the possession gained full Nisab amount then Zakat is due.
6. If one has Nisab amount with mixtures of halal and haram merchandise then Zakat is due.

7. Zakat must be calculated based on current price of merchandise and not the purchased price.
8. If one partner of a company has share equal or exceeds Nisab, then the partner must pay Zakat.
9. Stock must be calculated based on Islamic year and not fiscal year.
10. Zakat is Fard on current price of shares held in a company during each calendar year. Machinery, fixtures, furniture, buildings, Land, and liabilities are exempt from total assets. Zakat is due on the balance.
11. When Zakat is paid on an amount once and the same amount remains with the owner next full year, Zakat is due again. Zakat will be Fard repeatedly after every Islamic year.
12. If one did not pay Zakat on wealth at the end of year and all that wealth either lost or stolen, then Zakat is exempt. If wealth is deliberately lost or destroyed then Zakat is due.
13. If one gives away all his wealth to charity without Zakat niyat after a year, then that amount is exempt from Zakat. If part of the wealth is given away then the remainder of the wealth (if equals to Nisab) must be calculated to pay Zakat.

Chapter – 7: Adhia / Qurbani + Aquiqa

First 10 days of Zul Hajj

1. Ibn Abbas ؓ related that Rasul ﷺ said: On no other days are good deeds more liked by Allah than on these days – first 10 days of Zul Hajj. Sahaba ؓ asked O Rasulullah ﷺ: not even jihad for Allah? Rasul ﷺ replied: not even jihad for Allah except for that person who goes out to fight with his life, wealth and does not return with anything. *(Bukhari).*

2. Rasul ﷺ said: On no days the worship of Allah desired more than during the first 10 days of Zul Hajj. Fasting of each of these days is equal to the fast of a whole year, the worship of each of these nights is equal to the worship of Lailatul Qadr. *(Tirmizi, Ibn Maja).*

3. Ibn Abbas ؓ relates that Rasul ﷺ said: No days are as weighty and liked by Allah for good deeds than the first 10 days of Zul Hajj.

4. Recite: سُبْحَانَ الله اَلْحَمْدُ لِلّهِ لآ اِلهَ اِلاَّ اللهُ اَللهُ اَكْبَرُ

   Subhanallah alhamdulillal lailaha illallahu allahu akbar.

5. Abu Qatadah ؓ relates that Rasul ﷺ was asked about the fasting on Arafat day (9th Zul Hajj). He said: it compensates for the minor sins of past year and the coming year. *(Muslim).*

6. Rasul ﷺ said: the most acceptable du'a is that which is made on the day of Arafat and the best du'a which all past prophets have made is: لآ اِلهَ اِلاَّ الأَاللهُ وَحْدَهُ لاَشَرِيْكَ لَهُ لَهُ الْمُلْكُ وَلَهُ الْحَمْدُ وَهُوَ عَلَى كُلِّ شَىءٍ قَدِيْرٌ

   La ilaha illallahu wahdahu la sharika lahu lahul mulku walahul humdu wahua ala kulle shayyen qadeer. (There is no deity besides Allah, He is alone. He has no partner. He owns sovereignty and all praise, and He is all-powerful. *(Tirmizi).*

7. Maaz Ibn Jabal ؓ relates that Rasul ﷺ said: jannat is wajib for those who stay awake with the intention of making Ibadat on the nights of 8th, 9th and 10th of Zul Hajj, night of Eidul Fitr and 15th Saban.

Importance of Adhia / Qurbani

1. Qur'an says: It is not their meat, nor their blood that reaches Allah. It is your piety that reaches Him.

2. Rasul ﷺ said: There is nothing dearer to Allah during Qurbani days than the sacrifice of animals. The sacrificed animals on the Day of Judgment will be weighed as good deeds. Sacrifice is accepted to Allah before blood reaches the ground.

3. Rasul ﷺ said: The person who makes Qurbani for rewards from Allah, then on the day of judgment that Qurbani will shield him from the fires of hell. Each Muslim should take advantage of this opportunity and sacrifice as many as he can afford. The wealth should be used to make Nafl Qurbani for Rasul ﷺ, his ummat and for his own living or deceased relatives. Nafl Qurbani does not need permission.

Warning to Ignore Qurbani

Rasul ﷺ said that the person who has the means to do Qurbani but does not do so, should not even come near the place of Eid prayer.

Time for Qurbani

1. Time begins after Eid Salat on the 10th Zil Hajj and ends at sunset on 12th.
2. It is best to make Qurbani on the first day.
3. It is preferred to slaughter during the day.
4. It is OK to slaughter before Eid if there is no Eid Salat in the area.
5. If it is not sure whether it is 12th or 13th, better to give away all meat.
6. If an animals bought for Qurbani are not slaughtered during these days, it must be given away alive as charity.

Who must DO Qurbani

1. Qurbani is wajib on all Muslims (male and female) who are sane, proper age, possess minimum Nisab wealth.
2. Qurbani is wajib on a man for himself, not for his wife and children but should be made if they are owners of Nisab wealth with permission.
3. Qurbani is not required for poor people or travelers or minors.
4. Qurbani for a deceased is wajib if he had asked to do from his wealth.
5. If a person intends to do Qurbani after certain work is completed then Qurbani becomes wajib.
6. If a poor person buys an animal for Qurbani then it is wajib to sacrifice. If this animal dies or gets lost, Qurbani will not be wajib. If he buys another animal and the first one is found, it becomes wajib to sacrifice both animals.
7. If a person buys an animal for Qurbani because it is wajib on him and it is lost, stolen or died then it will be wajib to sacrifice another

one. If after buying 2nd animal, the first one is found, only one is wajib to sacrifice. He can sacrifice the 2nd one also.

8. If a person buys an animal for Qurbani because it is wajib on him and did not slaughter due to some reason on a fixed day, it is wajib on him to give the animal away as charity.

9. If a person on whom Qurbani is wajib failed to do for a number of years, should donate the value of number of animals as charity. Slaughtering several animals for missed years will not compensate missed years.

10. If a person performs Qurbani on behalf of another person on whom Qurbani is wajib without his permission or knowledge, Qurbani is not valid. If it is done with permission, it is OK.

11. It is mustahab for those who want to make Qurbani not to cut hair or clip nails from 1st Zil Hajj noon until after Qurbani.

Conditions for Qurbani Animals

1. Qurbani can only be made of goat, sheep, cattle and camel.

2. Castrated and barren animal is preferred.

3. Goat and sheep need to be at least one year old. Cattle must be at least 2 years old, camel must be 5 year old.

4. Sheep or goat counts as one share. Cattle or camel can be divided into 7 shares. Seven people can make Qurbani with one cow or camel.

5. If a person sacrifice one whole cow or camel, his wajib will be one share and the rest will be counted as Nafl / optional Qurbani.

6. If more then 7 persons share one cow or camel, Qurbani of all will be invalid.

7. Niyat of all 7 persons for cow or camel must be on Qurbani. If anyone has intention of merely eating meat, the Qurbani of all will be invalid.

8. It is OK to make intention to share 7 names when buying a cow or camel.

9. If one makes intention to use for himself during purchase of a cow or camel and then shares with others, then Qurbani of shareholders will be valid. Purchaser's Qurbani will be valid if he is rich. If he is poor, he will have to make Qurbani for that number of shares that he has given to others. If the days of Qurbani have passed, he must give the amount of shares to the poor.

10. Animal chosen for Qurbani should be healthy, free from defects.

Defective Animals NOT Allowed

1. Animal born without horns or horns broken from middle can be used. If horn is broken from root, can not be used.
2. Totally blind or lost 1/3rd or more eyesight, 1/3rd or more ear cut or tail cut are not allowed.
3. Animal, which limps and walks on 3 legs and cannot put injured 4th leg on ground cannot be used.
4. Animal without teeth cannot be used. Some missing teeth is OK.
5. Animal born without ears, very thin, weak, sick and unable to walk cannot be used.
6. If an animal sustains injury during slaughter or leg breaks or ear is cut, Qurbani is OK.
7. If the animal become injured after purchase for Qurbani, it is OK to use same animal if purchaser is not rich. If he is rich, then he must buy another one in place of the injured.
8. If an animal bought for Qurbani gives birth before slaughter, then newly born should also be slaughtered.

Qurbani Meat and Skin

1. It is OK for a person who performs Qurbani to either eat meat or give to anyone (rich or poor) Muslim or non-Muslim.
2. It is OK to divide meat into 3 parts – one for home, one for relatives and friends and one to poor and needy.
3. Meat or skin cannot be given to employee or butcher for work. It may be given as gift.
4. Skin can be kept for personal use or can be give to anyone.
5. Skin cannot be given for service even to Imam or Moazzin or anybody for their service.
6. If skin is sold, amount received cannot be used for himself but must give away as charity to poor or needy.
7. It is not OK to eat following types of Qurbani meat -
   • On Kaffara for error committed during Hajj.
   • On deceased person due to his wasiyat.
   • Due to vow one had made. This type of meat must be distributed to poor or needy.
8. Meat of Nafl Qurbani, which one had made for deceased, can be eaten by all.
9. If several persons share an animal (usually 7), then each share must be divided by weight. If one share of meat is less than the other but shin or head or leg is given, it is OK.

Slaughter of Qurbani Animals

1. It is mustahab to slaughter personally. If the owner is unable, he can delegate who can do in Islamic zabah / slaughter. It a person is delegated, that person should be present. Muslim women who know zabah can <u>also</u> slaughter.
2. Islamic zabah requires throat, external jugular veins and windpipe of animal be swiftly and clearly severed with a very sharp knife with the recitation of *bismillahi allahu akbar*. If only two of the passages and veins are cut, zabah will be incorrect.
3. It is mustahab to face qibla during slaughtering.
4. It is preferable to sharpen knife to ease suffering. Animal should not be skinned or cut into pieces before it turns completely cold.
5. An animal should not be slaughtered in presence of another animal.

Takbir of Tasriq

It is wajib for every adult Muslim to recite in audible tone (not silently nor very loudly) the following Takbir Tasriq once after every Fard Salat (performed in jamat) from Fajr Salat on the 9th Zil Hajj until after Asr Salat on 13th Zil Hajj (23 Salats).

اَللّٰهُ اَكْبَرُ اَللّٰهُ اَكْبَرُ لَاۤاِلٰهَ اِلَّا اللّٰهُ وَاللّٰهُ اَكْبَرُ اَللّٰهُ اَكْبَرُ وَلِلّٰهِ الْحَمْدُ

Allahu akbar allahu akbar lailaha illallahu aallahu akbar allahu akbar walillahel hamd. (Allah is great Allah is great. There is no deity besides Allah and Allah is great and all praise belongs to Him alone).

Sunnah of Eidul Adha

1. Wakeup earlier than usual, brush teeth with meswak and take bath.
2. Dress with best clothes (need not be new) in an Islamic manner.
3. Use itr / fragrance, avoid eating before Eid Salat, reach prayer place early and perform Eid Salat at large gathering.
4. Walk to the place of Eid prayer (if within walking distance) reciting takbirat aloud through one way and return through different route.

Sadqatul Fitr

1. It is wajib to pay Sadqatul Fitr upon one who pays Zakat.
2. If Zakat is due on a person but has not paid yet because Islamic year has not passed, Sadqatul Fitr is wajib on that person.
3. Sadqatul Fitr is due on a person, his wife and all his dependents. If dependent possesses wealth, Fitr can be given from their wealth.
4. If a child is born after Fajr on Eid day, Fitr is not wajib.

5. If Fitr is wajib, it must be paid whether he fasted in Ramadan or not.
6. If a person dies on Eid day before Fajr Salat, Fitr is not wajib.
7. It is preferred to pay Fitr before Eid Salat. If one did not pay on Eid day, he can pay on any time later.
8. The rate of Fitr is equivalent to the price of approximately 8.5 lbs of wheat, flour, bran, raisin, date or barley.
9. Recipient of Fitr is same as that of Zakat.
10. Fitr of one person can be given to one person or distributed to few persons. Similarly Fitr of several persons can be collectively be given to one person.

Aquiqa (of Animal for Newly Born Child and Removal of Head Hair)

1. Name a newborn child (male or female) on 7th day of birth. Sacrifice (Aquiqa) (preferably on the 7th day) as 2 goats or sheeps for boy and one goat or sheep for girl. If a cow or camel is chosen, 2 shares for boy and one share for girl should be used. Shave head hair and amount of silver equal to the hair weight should be given as charity (not compulsory).
2. Any animal not permitted for Qurbani can not be used for Aquiqa. It is OK to distribute meat of Aquiqa raw / cooked and can be served to guests.
3. If one does not have enough money, it is OK to use one goat / sheep for boy or does not perform Aquiqa.

Chapter – 8: Omrah + Hajj and Ziarat to Madinah

Virtues of Hajj
Hajj is the 5th pillar of Islam. Hajj means to visit Mecca during Hajj days (8-12th of Zil Hajj). Allah ﷻ says: Hajj is bounded duty whosoever disbelieves, then Allah is free and independent from the entire universe. *(Al-Imran: 97)*

Rasul ﷺ mentioned:
1. Allah has declared Hajj compulsory upon you, therefore perform Hajj.
2. Hasten in performing Hajj, for one never knows what will befall him.
3. One who dies while on Hajj journey, Allah will record the reward of Hajj up to the day of Qiyamah and one who dies while on Omrah journey, Allah will record the reward of Omrah up to the day of Qiyamah.
4. For an accepted Hajj, there is no reward besides paradise.
5. One who possesses wealth and has all the means by which he could reach the sacred house of Kaba and yet does not perform Hajj, then he may either die as a Christian or a fire worshipper.

Preconditions of Hajj: That a person be
1. Muslim.
2. Free person, not a slave.
3. Proper age with sound mind, not insane.
4. Has ability to provide boarding and lodging during journey.
5. Able to leave sufficiently for his family and children who stay behind during his absence.
6. If female, be accompanied by her husband or mahram during journey.
7. A woman is over her period of waiting after divorce.

Niyat of Hajj: Niyat must be made at the miqat (boundary which may not be crossed without Ihram).

Three types of Hajj can be performed with Ihram
1. **Mufrid** - Hajj only
2. **Qiran** - Hajj and Omrah with same Ihram: enter miqat with Ihram, perform Omrah: tawaf 7 times around Kaba (first 3 with jogging speed), proceed with the acts of Hajj.
3. **Tamattu (easiest Hajj)** - Hajj and Omrah with two separate Ihrams without leaving miqat: Enter Miqat with Ihram, perform Omrah: Tawaf seven times around Kaba, Perform Sae between Safa and Marwah, proceed with the acts of Hajj.

Omrah Requirements
Two Fard
1. Wear Ihram.
2. Complete tawaf at least 4 times.

Three Wajibs
1. Complete tawaf 7 times.
2. Sai / walk between Safa and Marwah.
3. Shave head hair or trim all sides equally.

Omrah Procedure
1. Put Ihram before entering Miqat / boundary.
2. Perform 2 rakats for Ihram.
3. Make niyat and say talbiyah constantly.
4. Proceed to Mecca.
5. Perform tawaf around Kaba.
6. Perform 2 rakats wajib Salat behind Maqame Ibrahim.
7. Proceed to Multazam and zam zam well.
8. Perform sai between Safa and Marwah.
9. Shave or trim hair.

Hajj Requirements

Three Fard: (must be complete during Hajj days. Any omission will make it compulsory to perform Hajj following year).
1. Be in Ihram.
2. Be present on the Arafat.
3. Perform final tawaf of Hajj.

Wajibs of Hajj: (require sacrifice as penalty one goat / sheep per omission to validate Hajj).
1. Stay night at Muzdalifah.
2. Walk 7 times between Safa and Marwah with Ihram.
3. Pelt pebbles (**Ramee**) at Jamrat in Mina.
4. Shave (**Halq**) head hair (for male).
5. For Qiran Hajj: sacrifice (**Nahr**) a sheep / goat within limits of Haram.
6. First Tawaf (**Tawafuz Ziarat**) for residents of Mecca.
7. Farewell Tawaf.

Sunnats of Hajj: (carry great reward. Any omission of Sunnah does not need penalty).
1. Gusl before Ihram.
2. Use fragrance before Ihram.
3. Use two sheets for Ihram.
4. Perform 2 rakats before Ihram.
5. Say Talbiyah, say loudly, and say 3 times together.

Ihram Process: Before Ihram:
1. Cut hair, public hair, nails.
2. Perform Gusl if possible otherwise make Wudu.
3. Wear Ihram.
4. Use slipper as footwear.
5. Perform 2 rakats of Nafl.
6. Recite talbiyah loudly and as frequently as possible.
7. Ihram must not be ended without completing Hajj or Omrah.

Ihram Dress
1. It must be worn from miqat.
2. It is best to use white color.
3. Upper piece should wrap around the body such that it goes below the right arm with right shoulder open to over the left shoulder.
4. Lower piece should be adequate to cover satr (required by Sariah).
5. This Ihram dress wearing method is called **Idtiba**.

Prohibited During Ihram
1. Bad or angry talk, argue.
2. Hunting and killing animals.
3. Sex, play games, sins.
4. Scratch body parts, use soap, and comb hair.
5. Remove dirt or hair from body, cut nails or hairs.
6. Use any itr / fragrance.
7. Cover face, cover head.
8. Wear sewn garment including underwear and sox.

Women Exceptions
1. Must wear normal dress as ihram but face must not be covered.
2. Women do not make Idtiba or ramal during tawaf.
3. Do not run between green lights during Sai.
4. Can not enter haram during menses.
5. Should not recite talbiyah loudly like men.

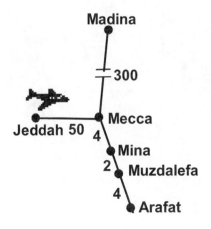

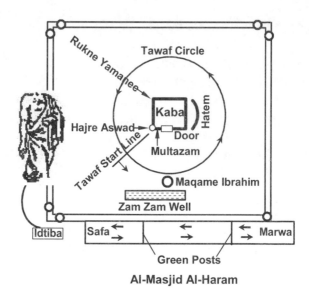

Al-Masjid Al-Haram

Hajj Steps

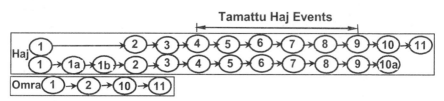

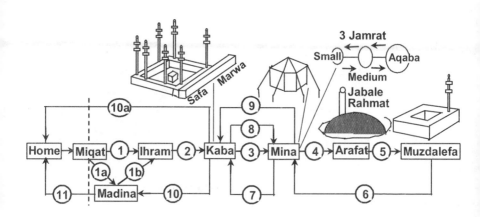

(1) **Ihram**
Clean yourself (gusl) and Wear Ihram clothes.
- Make Intention for Umrah and Recite Talbeyah.
- Avoid forbidden acts of Ihram.

(2) **Omra**
- Make Tawaf and Pray 2 rakat @ Maqame Ibrahim.
- Make Sai between Safa and Marwa.
- Trim hair and remove Ihram clothes.

(3) **Mecca to Mina (Noon, the 8th)**
- Put Ihram clothes again and Make Niah of Haj.
- Remain in Mina during Tarwiah day and perform 5 Prayers starting from Zohr salat and end with Fajr Salat on the day of Arafat (9th).

(4) **Mina to Arafat (Morning, the 9th)**
- Leave for Arafat on 9th morning and stay until sunset.
- Stay in Arafat and glorify Allah, repent to Allah and Ask for forgiveness.
- Pray zohr and Asr (shortened) *combined* at zohr

(5) **Arafat to Muzdalefa (after sunset, the 9th)**
- Leave for Muzdalefa after sunset on the 9th.
- Perform Magrib and Isa (shortened) *combined* at Isa time at Muzdalefa.
- Collect 70 stones for jamrat, stay overnight and perform Fajr

(6) **Muzdalefa to Mina (sunrise, the 10th)**
- Before sunrise pray Fajr, leave for Mina.
- Go to Jamrat and stone Aqaba (big) with 7 stones.
- Slaughter your sacrifice, Shave head or trim hair.
- Take off Ihram clothes, all restrictions are lifted.

(7) **Tawaf Al-Ifada (10' or after)**
- Make Tawaf Al Ifada, make Sai between Safa and Marwa.
- All restrictions are lifted.

(8) **Mecca to Mina (the 10th, 11th, 12th, 13th)**
- Spend the Tashreeq days in Mina.
- After Zohr each day, stone three Jamarat, starting from small and finish with Aqaba (21 each for 11th, 12th and 13th) (Sunnat to pelt from Zawal to sunset)
- You may leave on 12th after stoning Jamarat.

(9) **Farewell Tawaf (after the 12th)**
- Go to Mecca and make farewell Tawaf.
- Perform 2 rakat of Tawaf.
- Let Tawaf be the last thing you do in Mecca.

(1a) (1b) (10) (10a) (11)
Madina Monwara Visit (optional)
- It is preferred to visit the Masjid Nabubi in Madina, but it is not part of Haj.
- If you visit before Haj, follow 1a, 1b and 10a.
- If you visit after Haj, follow 10 and 11.
- Recite Durud, pray at Riazul Jannah, and visit Jannatul Baki.

Du'a, Du'a and Du'a….

- Abu Huraira 🕮 reports from Rasulullah 🕮 that the Hajji and Mutamir are guests of Allah. When they make du'a to Him, He accepts, and when they seek His pardon, He forgives them.
- Ibn Abbas 🕮 relates from Rasul 🕮 that 5 types of Du'as are accepted:
  1. The call of the oppressed until assisted.
  2. The prayer of the Hajji until he returns.
  3. The Mujahid until completed (Jihad).
  4. The call of the sick until recovered.
  5. The prayer of a fellow Muslim for his absent brother.

Etiquette of Du'a
1. Du'as are not accepted if earnings are haram / unlawful.
2. Wherever possible, face Qibla.
3. Recite du'a in a moderate tone.
4. Be humble and imploring to Allah.
5. Repeat du'a 3 times.
6. Hope for acceptance but do not expect immediate results.
7. Be attentive while making du'a.
8. Begin every du'a praising Allah, send salam to Rasul 🕮, end prayer with Durud and praise of Allah.
9. Include repentance.
10. Settle any outstanding wrong doings with others.
11. Turn towards Allah only.

Times when Du'as are accepted
1. Friday.
2. Last third portion of the night.
3. When it rains.
4. When Salat is about to start and after Salat.
5. When Kaba is seen.

Places where Du'as are accepted
1. Arafat on the 9th of Zil Hajj.
2. Mina (especially after stoning the 1st and 2nd jam rats on the 11th and 12th of Zil Hajj).
3. At Multazam.
4. At Zam Zam well.
5. Safa -Marwah and in between the two.
6. At Kaba.

7. At Hateem.
8. At Rukne Yamane.
9. At Hajjre Aswad.
10. Muzdalifah - last portion of night and between Fajr azan and sunrise.

Du'as at Different Steps of Hajj / Omrah

1. Ihram Process:
Make niyat and recite Talbiyah constantly.

1A. Niyat of Hajj (after wearing Ihram before miqat):

اَللّٰهُمَّ اِنِّیْ اُرِیْدُ الْحَجَّ فَیَسِّرْهُ لِیْ وَتَقَبَّلْهَا مِنِّیْ

Allahumma inni oredul hajja fayassirhu li wataqaballahu minni (O Allah I make a niyat to perform Hajj, hence make this Ibadat easy for me and accept it from me).

1B. Talbiyah
(constantly recite after Ihram, mustahab to say 3 times together):

لَبَّیْكَ اللّٰهُمَّ لَبَّیْكَ لَبَّیْكَ لَاشَرِیْكَ لَكَ لَبَّیْكَ اِنَّ الْحَمْدَ وَالنِّعْمَةَ لَكَ وَالْمُلْكَ لَاشَرِیْكَ لَكَ

Labbayak allahumma Labbayak, Labbayak la sharikalaka Labbayak innalhamda wannaimatalaka walmulk. lasharikalaka. (Here I am at Your service O Allah, I am present, I am present, You have no partner, I am present. All praise and graciousness as well as the entire universe is Yours, You have no partner).

2. Tawaf Process
Enter Kaba (with right foot in first through any door) and recite du'a.

2A. Du'a to Enter Kaba: اللّٰهُمَّ افْتَحْ لِیْ اَبْوَابَ رَحْمَتِكَ
Allahumma aftahli abwaba rahmatika
(O Allah, open for us the doors of Your mercy).

2B. Du'a when you see Kaba:

اَللّٰهُمَّ اَنْتَ السَّلَامُ وَمِنْكَ السَّلَامُ ـ فَحَیِّنَا رَبَّنَا بِالسَّلَامِ اللّٰهُمَّ زِدْ هٰذَا تَعْظِیْمًا وَّتَشْرِیْقًا وَّتَكْرِیْمًا وَّمَهَابَةً ـ وَزِدْ مَنْ حَجَّهُ اَوِ اعْتَمَرَ تَشْرِیْقًا وَّتَكْرِیْمًا وَّتَعْظِیْمًا وَّبِرًّا

Allahumma antassalam waminkassalam. fahiyana rabbana bessalam. allahumma zedbytaka haza tawzimao wattashrifao watakrimao wamahabatan. wazedmun hajjahu awatamara tashrifao watakrimao watazimao waberun. (O Allah, You are peace and from you is peace, therefore keep us alive with peace. O Allah, increase this house of Yours with reverence, dignity, honor and respect; and increase those who perform Hajj or Omrah towards it in dignity, honor, reverence, obedience and righteousness).

If any Fard Salat is about to begin, pray and then start tawaf.

2C. Niyat of Tawaf: (make Idtiba / see figure i.e. cover body, left shoulder, left arm and back are covered and right arm is entirely open):

اَللّٰهُمَّ اِنِّىْ اُرِيْدُ طَوَافَ بَيْتِكَ الْحَرَام فَيَسِّرْهُ لِىْ وَتَقَبَّلْهُ مِنِّى سَبْعَةَ اَشْوَاطٍ لِلّٰهِ تَعَالٰى عَزَّ وَجَلَّ

Allahumma inni uridu tawafa baitekal harame fayassirhu li watakabbalhu minni sabaata ashwati lillahe taala azwajalla. (O Allah, I intend to perform Sai between Safa and Marwah 7 circles for Allah, make it easy for me and accept it from me).

- Start from Haze Aswad line with du'a counter clockwise with left shoulder facing Kaba (*see figure for Idtiba*),
- Raise both hands to ears like Salat and say du'a, lower hands, make **Istilam** (kissing of stone) if possible or stretch your palms towards Hazre Aswad and back of hands towards face, kiss palms.

2D. Du'a During Tawaf

اَللّٰهُمَّ قَنِّعْنِىْ بِمَا رَزَقْتَنِىْ وَبَارِكْ لِىْ فِيْهِ وَاخْلُفْ عَلٰى كُلِّ غَائِبَةٍ لِىْ بِخَيْرٍ لَا اِلٰهَ اِلاَّ اللهُ وَحْدَهُ لاَشَرِيْكَ لَهُ ـ لَهُ الْمُلْكُ وَلَهُ الْحَمْدُ وَهُوَ عَلٰى كُلِّ شَيْءٍ قَدِيْرٌ

Allahumma qannini bima razaqtani wabarekli fihe wakhluf alakulle gaaibatilli bekhairen lailaha illallahu wahdahu lasharikalahu lahulmulku walahul hamdu wahua ala kulle shaiyen qadir. (O Allah, give me contentment in that which You have provided for me, and bestow me with Barakat therein, and be a successor of all whom I have left behind. There is no deity except Allah, He is alone, He has no partner, the universe belongs solely to Him, and all praise is solely for Him, He alone gives life and death, in His hand lies all the good, and He has infinite power over everything).

رَبَّنَا اٰتِنَا فِىْ الدُّنْيَا حَسَنَةً وَّفِىْ الْاٰخِرَةِ حَسَنَةً وَّقِنَا عَذَابَ النَّار

Rabbana atena fidduniya hasanatao wafil akherate hasanatao waqena azabannar. (O Allah, grant us goodness in this world and goodness in the hereafter and save us from the punishment of the fire).

سُبْحَانَ اللهِ وَالْحَمْدُ لِلّٰهِ وَلَا اِلٰهَ اِلاَّ اللهُ وَاللهُ اَكْبَرُ وَلاَحَوْلَ وَلاَقُوَّةَ اِلاَّ بِاللهِ الْعَلِىّ الْعَظِيْمِ

Subhanallahe walhamdulillahe walailaha illallahu wallahu akbar. walahaula walakuwata illabillahel aliul azim. (Allah is free from every imperfection and impurity, and everything derogatory from His glory, and all praise is due to Allah, and there is no deity worth of worship besides Allah, and Allah is the greatest, and there is no strength, nor power but with Allah, the Highest and Greatest).

- Turn 7 rounds (**ramal** - walking hastily during first 3 rounds).
- Pray 2 rakats (wajib) at **Maqame Ibrahim** and make du'a.
- Go to Zam Zam well and drink water as much as you can standing and facing Kaba.

2E. Du'a After Drinking Zam Zam water

اللَّهُمَّ اِنِّيْ اَسْئَلُكَ عِلْمًا نَافِعًا وَّرِزْقًا وَّاسِعًا وَّشِفَاءً مِّنْ كُلِّ دَاءٍ

Allahumma inni asaluka elmun nafeau warezkau wasiao washifaao minkulledaa. (O Allah, I am asking You for beneficial knowledge, and abundance in provision, and cure from every ailment).

Go to **Multazam** (if you can), cling and make du'a.

2F. Du'a at Hajre Aswad: اللهُ اَكْبَرُ - لَااِلهَ اِلَّا اللهُ

allahu akbar lailaha illallahu.
(Allah is great, there is no deity besides Allah).

3. Sai Process:
- Start from Safa with niyat,
- Raise hands facing Kaba and say Allahu Akbar and du'a,

3A. Du'a Before starting Sai after Safa

اللَّهُمَّ اِنِّيْ اُرِدُّ السَّعْىَ بَيْنَ الصَّفَا وَالْمَرْوَةَ سَبْعَةَ اَشْوَاطٍ لِلّهِ عَزَّ وَجَلَّ فَيَسِّرْهُ لِىْ وَتَقَبَّلْهُ مِنِّىْ

Allahumma inni uridussaia bynassafa walmarwata sabata ashwate lillahe azza wajalla fayasseruhu li watakabbalhu minni.(O Allah, I intend to perform Sai between Safa and Marwah 7 circles for Allah, make it easy for me and accept it from me).

- Walk faster between green posts, from Marwah to Safa completes one round.
- Make 7 rounds with du'a, zikr and Durud.

3B. After Sai recite du'a

لَا اِلهَ اِلَّا اللهُ وَحْدَهُ لَاشَرِيْكَ لَهُ لَهُ الْمُلْكُ وَلَهُ الْحَمْدُ يُحْيِى وَيُمِيْتُ وَهُوَ عَلَى كُلِّ شَىءٍ قَدِيْرٌ - لَا اِلهَ اِلَّا اللهُ وَحْدَهُ- اَنْجَزَ وَعْدَهُ وَنَصَرَ عَبْدَهُ -وَهَزَمَ الْاَحْزَابَ وَحْدَهُ

La ilaha illallahu wahdahu lasarikalahu lahulmulku walahul hamdu yuhyi waumitu wahua ala kulle shaiyan qadir. lailaha illallahu wahdahu waumitu wahua ala kulle shaiyan qadir. lailaha illallahu wahdahu anjaza wadahu wanasara abduhu wahazama ahzaba wahdahu. (There is no deity besides Allah, He is alone, He has no partner, the universe belongs only to Him, and all praise is solely for Him, he alone gives life and death, He has infinite power over everything. There is no deity but Allah alone, He has fulfilled His promise, He aided His servant (Muhammad ﷺ and defeated all allies all alone).

- It is mustahab to perform 2 rakats in haram.
- Shave head or trim hair.
- Women must trim slightly more than an inch from the end.

After Hajj
1. Make niyat for more pious life
2. Do not complain about hardship, heat, local people of holy places.
3. Make sincere intention of Hajj for Allah only.
4. Sign of mabroor / accepted Hajj is when he / she returns, life changes for the better.

Visit Madina Monawara

1. Visit of Rasul's ﷺ grave is the highest of mustahab acts.
2. Recite Durud as much as possible and whenever you can.
3. It is of great merit to enter through the door **Babe Gibrail**.
4. Inside the Masjid, if it is Fard Salat time, perform Salat. Perform 2 rakat Tahiyatul Masjid in the **Rawdah / Riazul Jannah.**

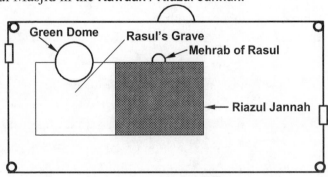

Masjide Nabubi

5. Rasul ﷺ said: Between my home and my Mimbar is a garden of the gardens of Jannah.
6. It is <u>best</u> to perform 2 rakat Tahiyatul Masjid in the Mehrab of Rasul ﷺ. Proceed very carefully with great respect and eagerness in mind to the Qadr of Rasul ﷺ.
7. Stand in front of Qadr under the green dome area with your back towards Qibla.
8. Do not cast your gaze all over or raise your voice.
9. Adapt an attitude of utmost respect.
10. Do not do anything disrespectful.
11. Do not stand very close to the holy Qadr.
12. Do not touch the wire-mesh enclosure, kiss or make sejda.
13. While standing, say Salam in a moderate tone like:

Assalamu Alaikum Ya Rasulullah ﷺ. السَّلَامُ عَلَيْكَ يَا رَسُوْلَ اللهِ

(Salam upon you, O Rasulullah)
14. Rasul ﷺ said: If anyone says salam in front of my grave, I can hear Salam.
15. After salam, make du'a to Allah and request for safat / intercession of Rasul ﷺ.
16. Move slightly to right standing and recite salam on Abu Bakr ﷺ.

17. On the right of Abu Bakr ◌, is the grave of Omar ◌. Recite Salam on Omar ◌.
18. Stay inside Masjid with niyat of Nafl I'tikaf.
19. Try to give sadqa to local poor Muslims.
20. Never make your back towards the holy grave while in Madina.
21. It is mustahab to visit Jannatul Baki where important companions and family members of Rasul ﷺ have their graves.

An important du'a of Rasul ﷺ

اللّٰهُمَّ اِنَّكَ تَسْمَعُ كَلَامِىْ وَنَرَى مَكَانِى وَتَعْلَمُ سِرِّىْ وَعَلَا نِيَتِىْ وَلَايَخْفٰى عَلَيْكَ
شَيْئٌ مِّنْ اَمْرِىْ وَاَنَا الْبَائِسُ الْفَقِيْرُ الْمُسْتَغِيْثُ الْمُسْتَجِيْرُ الْوَجِلُ الْمُشْفِقُ الْمُقِرُّ
الْمُعْتَرِفُ بِذَنبِى اِسْئَلُكَ مَسْئَلَةَ الْمِسْكِيْنِ وَاَبْتَهِلُ اِلَيْكَ اِبْتِهَالَ الْمُذْنِبِ الذَّلِيْلِ
وَاَدْعُوْكَ دُعَاءَ الْخَائِفِ الضَّرِيْرِ وَدُعَاءَ مَنْ خَضَعَتْ لَكَ رَقَبَتُهُ وَفَاضَمَتُ لَكَ
عَبْرَتُهُ وَذَلَّ لَكَ جِيْسَمُهُ وَرَغِمَ لَكَ اَنْفُهُ اللّٰهُمَّ لَاتَجْعَلْنِى بِدُعَائِكَ شَقِيًّا وَكُّنْ لِّى رَؤُفًا
رَّحِيْمًا يَاخَيْرَ الْمَسْئُوْلِيْنَ وَيَا خَيْرَ الْمُعْطِيْنَ

Allahumma innaka tasmau kalahimi watara makaniu watalamu sirriyu wala niyati wala yakhfa alaika shaiyum minamri wanal baesul faqirul mustaghisul mustajirul wajilul mushfiqul muqirul mutarefu bezumbi asaluka musalatal miskine wabtahelu ilaika ibtehalul miznebel zalile waduka duaal khaefed darire waduwaa mun khadaatlaka raqabatuhu wafadatlaka abratuhu wazallalaka jismuhu waraghemalaka anfuhu allahumma la tajalni bewuaeka shaqiau wakullirau farrahimun yakhairul musulina waya khairal muotina. (O my Allah! You listen to my speech and You see my condition and position, You are aware of me which is concealed and evident. None of my matters are hidden from You. I am afflicted with hardship and distress, needy (of Your threshold). I lodge my complaints only to You, I seek only Your protection, I am overcome by Your fear, I acknowledge and accept my sins and shortcomings. I beg You like that destitute who has no support and is lonely. I pled in Your presence like a disgraced sinner. I pray to You, the prayer of one who is overcome with Your fear and is afflicted with pain and distress, like the prayer of one whose head is hung down before You and whose tears are flowing in Your presence, whose body is humbled before You and rubbing his nose before You. O Allah! Do not reject my prayer and deprive me and be beneficent to me and have mercy upon me, O He who is the best and the greatest deity, O He who is the most generous).

Chapter – 9: 10 Suras + Different Du'as + Different Etiquette

Sura Fateha (The Opening): سُوْرَةُ الْفَاتِحَه مَكِّيَّةٌ

بِسْمِ اللهِ الرَّحْمنِ الرَّحِيْمِ – اَلْحَمْدُ لِلّهِ رَبِّ الْعلمِيْنَ – الرَّحْمنِ الرَّحِيْمِ – ملِكِ يَوْمِ
الدِّيْنِ – اِيَّاكَ نَعْبُدُ وَاِيَّاكَ نَسْتَعِيْنَ – اِهْدِنَا الصِّرَاطَ الْمُسْتَقِيْمَ – صِرَاطَ الَّذِيْنَ
اَنْعَمْتَ عَلَيْهِمْ غَيْرِ الْمَغْضُوْبِ عَلَيْهِمْ وَلَاالضَّالِّيْنَ –

Bismillaher Rahmaner Rahim. Alhamdulillahe Rabbil Alamin.
Arrahmaner Rahim. Maliki Yaomeddin. Iyya Kanabudu Wa Iyya
Kanastain. Ehdinus Seratal Mustaqim. Seratallazina An Amta Alaihim
Ghairil Mughdube Alaihim Waddaalin. Amin.

(In the name of Allah, the Most Beneficent, the Most Merciful. All the
praises and thanks be to Allah, the Lord of the Alamin (mankind, jinns
and all that exists) The Most Beneficent, the Most Merciful. The Only
Owner (and the Only Ruling Judge) of the Day of Resurrection. You
(alone) we worship, and You (alone) we ask for help (for each and
everything). Guide us to the Straight Way. The Way of those on whom
You have bestowed Your Grace, not (the way) of those who earned
Your Anger, nor of those who went astray).

Sura Nas (The Mankind): سُوْرَةُ النَّاس مَكِّيَّةٌ

بِسْمِ اللهِ الرَّحْمنِ الرَّحِيْمِ – قُلْ اَعُوْذُ بِرَبِّ النَّاس – مَلِكِ النَّاس – اِلهِ النَّاس –
مِنْ شَرِّ الْوَسْوَاسِ الْخَنَّاس – الَّذِيْ يُوَسْوِسُ فِيْ صُدُوْرِالنَّاس – مِنَ الْجِنَّةِ
وَالنَّاس –

Bismillaher Rahmaner Rahim. Qul Auzuberabbin Nas Malikin Nas
Elahin Nas. Min Sharril Waswasil Khannas. Allazi You Waswesu Fi
Sudurin Nas. Minul Jinnate Wan Nas.

(In the name of Allah, the Most Beneficent, the Most Merciful. Say: I
seek refuge with (Allah) the Lord of mankind, The King of mankind,
The Ilah (God) of mankind, From the evil of the whisperer (devil who
whispers evil in the hearts of men) who withdraws (from his
whispering in one's heart after one remembers Allah), Who whispers
in the breasts of mankind, Of jinns and men).

Sura Falak (The Day Break): سُوْرَةُ الْفَلَقِ مَكِّيَّةٌ

بِسْمِ اللهِ الرَّحْمنِ الرَّحِيْمِ – قُلْ اَعُوْذُ بِرَبِّ الْفَلَقِ – مِنْ شَرِّمَا خَلَقَ – وَمِنْ
شَرِّغَاسِقٍ اِذَا وَقَبَ – وَمِنْ شَرِّ النَّفَّثتِ فِى الْعُقَدِ – وَمِنْ شَرِّحَاسِدٍ اِذَا حَسَدَ –

Bismillaher Rahmaner Rahim. Qul Auzuberabbil Falaq. Min sharrema
Khalak. Wamin Sharre Ghasikin Iza waqab. Wamin Sharre Ha Sidin
Iza Hasad.

(In the name of Allah, the Most Beneficent, the Most Merciful. Say: I seek refuge with (Allah) the Lord of the day-break, From the evil of what He has created; And from the evil of the darkening (night) as it comes with its darkness; (or the moon as it sets or goes away). And from the evil of the witchcrafts when they blow in the knots, And from the evil of the envier when he envies).

Sura Ikhlas (The Purity): سُوْرَةُ الْإِخْلَاص مَكِّيَّة

بِسْمِ اللهِ الرَّحْمنِ الرَّحِيْمِ — قُلْ هُوَ اللهُ اَحَدٌ — اَللهُ الصَّمَدُ — لَمْ يَلِدْه وَلَمْ يُوْلَدْ — وَلَمْ يَكُنْ لَهُ كُفُوًا اَحَدٌ

Bismillaher Rahmaner Rahim. Qul Huallahu Ahad. Allahus Samad. Lam Yalid Walum Youlad. Walum Ya Kullahu Kufuwan Ahad.

(In the name of Allah, the Most Beneficent, the Most Merciful. Say (O Muhammad ﷺ): He is Allah, the (One). Allah is Samad (The Self-Sufficient Master, Whom all creatures need, He neither eats nor drinks). He begets not, nor was He begotten, And there is none co-equal or comparable unto Him).

Sura Al-Masad (The Palm Fibre): سُوْرَةُ اللّهَبِ مَكِّيَّة

بِسْمِ اللهِ الرَّحْمنِ الرَّحِيْمِ — تَبَّتْ يَدَا اَبِىْ لَهَبٍ وَتَبَّ — مَا اَغْنى عَنْهُ مَالُه وَمَا كَسَبَ — سَيَصْلى نَارًا ذَاتَ لَهَبٍ — وَامْرَاَتُه حَمَّالَةَ الْحَطَبِ — فِىْ جِيْدِهَا حَبْلٌ مِّنْ مَّسَدٍ

Bismillaher Rahmaner Rahim. Tabbat Yada Abila Habeu Watabba. Ma Aghna Anhu Maluhu Wama Kasab. Sayasla Narun zata Laha beo Wamraatuhu. Hamma Latul Hatab. Figi Deha Hublum Mimmasad.

(In the name of Allah, the Most Beneficent, the Most Merciful. Perish the two hands of Abu Lahab (an uncle of the Prophet), and perish he!. His wealth and his children (etc.) will not benefit him. He will be burnt in a fire of blazing flames! And his wife too, who carries wood (thorns of Sadan which she used to put on the way of the Prophet (ﷺ), or use to slander him). In her neck is a twisted rope of Masad (palm fibre)).

Sura An-Nasr (The Help): سُوْرَةُ النَّصْر مَكِّيَّة

بِسْمِ اللهِ الرَّحْمنِ الرَّحِيْمِ — اِذَاجَاءَ نَصْرُ اللهِ وَالْفَتْحُ — وَرَاَيْتَ النَّاسَ يَدْخُلُوْنَ فِىْ دِيْنِ اللهِ اَفْوَاجًا — فَسَبِّحْ بِحَمْدِ رَبِّكَ وَاسْتَغْفِرْه اِنَّه كَانَ تَوَابًا

Bismillaher Rahmaner Rahim. Iza Ja Anasullahe wal Fathu. Wara Eitanna Sayad Khuluna Fidinillahe Afwaja. Fasabbeh Behumde Rabbika Watugferhu Innahu Kaana Tauwaba.

(In the name of Allah, the Most Beneficent, the Most Merciful. When comes the Help of Allah (to you, O Muhammad (ﷺ) against your enemies) and the conquest (of Makka), And you see that the people enter Allah's Religion (Islam) in crowds, So glorify the Praises of your Lord, and ask for His Forgiveness. Verily, He is the One Who accepts the repentance and forgives).

Sura Al-Kafirun (The Disbelievers): سُوْرَةُ الْكَفِرُوْ مَكِّيَّة

بِسْمِ اللهِ الرَّحْمن الرَّحِيْم – قُلْ يَأَيُّهَا الْكَفِرُوْنَ – لاَاعْبُدُ مَاتَعْبُدُوْنَ – وَلاَ اَنْتُمْ عَبِدُوْنَ مَااعْبُدُ – وَلاَ اَنَا عَابِدُ مَّاعَبَدْتُمْ – وَلاَ اَنْتُمْ عَبِدُوْنَ مَا اعْبُدُ – لَكُمْ دِيْنُكُمْ وَلِىَ دِيْن

Bismillaher Rahmaner Rahim. Qul Ya Ayyuhal Kaferun. La Aabudu Ma Taahudun. Walantum Aabeduna Maabud. Wala Ana Abedumma Abattum. Walantum Aabeduna Maabud. Lakum Dinukun Walia Deen.

(In the name of Allah, the Most Beneficent, the Most Merciful. Say (Muhammad (ﷺ)): O Al-Kafirun (disbelievers in Allah, In His Oneness, in His Angels, in His Books, in His Messengers, in the Day of Resurrection, in Al-Qadar, etc.)! I worship not that which you worship, Nor will you worship that which I worship. And I shall not worship that which you are worshipping. Nor will you worship that which I worship. To you be your religion, and to me my religion (Islamic Monotheism)).

Sura Al- Kauther (A River in Paradise): سُوْرَةُ الْكَوْثِرْ مَكِّيَّة

بِسْمِ اللهِ الرَّحْمن الرَّحِيْم – اِنَّا اَعْطَيْنَكَ الْكَوْثَرَ – فَصَلِّ لِرَبِّكَ وَانْحَرْ – اِنَّ شَانِئَكَ هُوَ الْاَبْتَرْ

Bismillaher Rahmaner Rahim. Inna Aataina Kalkaosar. Fasalle Lerabbika Wanhur. Inna Shaniyaka Hual Abtar.

(In the name of Allah, the Most Beneficent, the Most Merciful. Verily, We have granted you (O Muhammad (ﷺ)) Al-Kauther; (a river in Paradise) Therefore turn in prayer to your Lord and sacrifice (to Him only). For he who makes you angry (O Muhammad (ﷺ)), - he will be cut off (from every good thing in this world and in the hereafter)).

Sura Al-Maun (The Small Kindnesses): سُوْرَةُ الْمَاعُوْن مَكِّيَّة

بِسْمِ اللهِ الرَّحْمن الرَّحِيْم – اَرَءَيْتَ الَّذِىْ يُكَذِّبُ بِالدِّيْن – فَذلِكَ الَّذِىْ يَدُعُ الْيَتِيْمَ – وَلَايَحُضُّ عَلى طَعَام الْمِسْكِيْن – فَوَيْلٌ لِّلْمُصَلِّيْنَ – الَّذِيْنَ هُمْ عَنْ صَلَاتِهِمْ سَاهُوْنَ – الَّذِيْنَ هُمْ يُرَاؤُوْنَ – وَيَمْنَعُوْنَ الْمَاعُوْنَ

Bismillaher Rahmaner Rahim. Ara Aytallazi You Kazzebubiddin. Fadale Kallazi Ya Doolyatim. Walaya Hudduala Tua Milmiskin. Fawailullil Musallina Allazina Hum Ansalatehim Saahun. Allazina Hum You Raoona Waium Naoonul Maoon.

(In the name of Allah, the Most Beneficent, the Most Merciful. Have you seen him who denies the Recompense? That is he who repulses the orphan (harshly), And urges not the feeding of the poor, So woe unto those performers of prayers (hypocrites), Who delay their prayer from its stated fixed time, Those who do good deeds only to be seen (of men), And refuse Al-Maun (small kindnesses e.g. salt, sugar, water, etc.)

Sura Quraish (Quraish): سُوْرَةُ قُرَيْشٍ مَكِّيَّةٌ

بِسْمِ اللهِ الرَّحْمنِ الرَّحِيْمِ – لاِيْلَفِ قُرَيْشٍ – اِلفِهِمْ رِحْلَة الشِّتَاءِ وَالصَّيْفِ –
– فَلْيَعْبُدُوْا رَبَّ هذَ الْبَيْتِ – الَّذِىْ اَطْعَمَهُمْ مِّنْ جُوْعٍ وَءَامَنَهُمْ مِّنْ خَوْفٍ

Bismillaher Rahmaner Rahim. Leilafe Quraisin Ilafehim. Rehlatusshiae Wassaif. Fulyabudu Rabba Hajal Baitillazi Atwamahum. Minjueo. Waamanahum Min Khaoof.

(In the name of Allah, the Most Beneficent, the Most Merciful. (It is a great Grace and Protection from Allah), for the taming of the Quraish, (And with all those Allah's Grace and Protections for their taming, We cause) the (Quraish) caravans to set forth safe in winter (to the south) and in summer (to the north without any fear),- So let them worship (Allah) the Lord of this House (the *Kaba* in Makka). (He) Who has fed them against hunger, and has made them safe from fear).

Sura Al-Fil (The Elephant): سُوْرَةُ الْفِيْلِ مَكِّيَّةٌ

بِسْمِ اللهِ الرَّحْمنِ الرَّحِيْمِ – اَلَمْ تَرَكَيْفَ فَعَلَ رَبُّكَ بِاَصْحبِ الْفِيْلِ – اَلَمْ يَجْعَلْ
كَيْدَهُمْ فِىْ تَضْلِيْلٍ – وَّاَرْسَلَ عَلَيْهمْ طَيْرًا اَبَابِيْلَ – تَرْمِيْهمْ بِحِجَارَةٍ مِّنْ سِجِّيْلٍ –
– فَجَعَلَهُمْ كَعَصْفٍ مَّاكُوْلٍ

Bismillaher Rahmaner Rahim. Alamtara Kaifa Faala Rabbuka Biashabil Feel. Alam yajal Kaida Hum Fi Tudlileo Waarsala Alaihim Tairan Ababil. Turmihi Beheja Ratim Minsijjilin Fajaada hum Kaasfim Maakul.

(In the name of Allah, the Most Beneficent, the Most Merciful. Have you (O Muhammad (ﷺ)) not seen how your Lord dealt with the owners of the elephant? [The elephant army which came from Yemen under the command of Abraha Al-Ashram intending to destroy the *Kaba* at Makka]. Did He not make their plot go astray? And send against them birds, in flocks, Striking them with stones of Sijjil. And made them like an empty field of stalks (of which the corn has been eaten up by cattle)).

Different Mosnun Du'as

There are many Mosnun Du'as for use in *everyday*. The following important Du'as are collected and listed in *four different groups* in certain sequence to easily identify and use them:

You Only
You + Others
Masjid Related
Travel Related

A1: Start Anything: بِسْمِ اللهِ الرَّحْمنِ الرَّحِيْمِ
Bismillaher Rahmaner Rahim. (In the name of Allah, the most Beneficent, the most Merciful)

A2: Intend to do Something: إِنْشَاءَ الله
Insallah. (If Allah will)

A3: Praise Something: سُبْحَانَ الله
Subhanallah (Glory be to Allah)

A4: Bathroom In: اَللَّهُمَّ إِنِّى أَعُوْذُبِكَ مِنَ الْخُبْثِ وَالْخَبَا ئِثِ
Allahumma Inni Auzubeka Minal Khubse Wal Khabaese.
(O Allah! I seek refuge with You from Satan, male or female).

A5: Bathroom Out: غُفْرَانَكَ اَلْحَمْدُ للهِ الَّذِى أَذْهَبَ عَنِّى الاَذى وَعَافَانِى
Ghufranaka Alhamdu Lillahellazi Azhaba Annal Aza Waafani.
(Your forgiveness, O Allah! All praise to Allah who has relieved me of distress and made me secure).

A6: Wudu start: اَللَّهُمَّ اغْفِرْ لِىْ ذَنْبِىْ وَوَسِّعْ لِى فِى دَارِىْ وَبَارِكْ لِى فِىْ رَزْقِىْ
Allahummagfirli zanbi Wawassili Fidaari Wabarikli Firrizqi. (O Allah! Forgive my sins and give expansion abundance in my home and grant me blessings in my sustenance).

A7: Wudu Finish: اَشْهَدُ اَنْ لاَّ اِلهَ اِلاَّ اللهُ وَاَشْهَدُ اَنَّ مُحَمَّدًا عَبْدُهُ وَرَسُوْلُهُ
Ash-hadu Allailaha Illallahu Wash-haduanna Muhammadan Abduhu Warasuluhu. (I testify that there is none worthy of worship but Allah, and I testify that Muhammad (ﷺ) is Allah's worshipper and messenger).

A8: Three Tasbih

1. 4ᵗʰ Kalema: سُبْحَانَ اللهِ وَالْحَمْدُ لِلهِ وَلاَاِلهَ اِلاَّ اللهُ وَاللهُ اَكْبَرُ وَلاَحَوْلَ وَلاَقُوَّةَ اِلاَّ بِاللهِ الْعَلِى الْعَظِيْمِ

Subhanallahe Walhamdulillahe Walailaha Illallahu Wallahuakbar Walahaola Walakuwata Illabillahel Alielazim. (Glory be to Allah. All praise be to Allah. There is none worthy of worship besides Allah. And Allah is the greatest. There is no power and might except from Allah. The most high -The great).

2. Short Durud sarif: اَللّٰهُمَّ صَلِّ عَلٰى سَيِّدِنَا مُحَمَّدٍ وَعَلٰى الِ سَيِّدِنَا مُحَمَّدٍ وَّبَارِكْ وَسَلِّمْ

Allahumma Salleala Sayedena Muhammadeo Walaale Sayedena Muhammadeo Wabarek Wasallam.

((O Allah! Shower Your mercy on Muhammad (ﷺ) and the followers of Muhammad (ﷺ)).

3. Astagfer: اَسْتَغْفِرُ اللهِ

Astagfirullah (I ask Allah to forgive my sins).

A9: After Every Salat: سُبْحَانَ اللهِ
Subhanallah 33 times,
اَلْحَمْدُ لِلّٰهِ *Alhamdu lillah* 33 times,
اللهُ اَكْبَرُ *Allahu Akbar* 34 times.

A10: Lailatul Qadr: اَللّٰهُمَّ اِنَّكَ عُفُوٌّ تُحِبُّ الْعَفْوَفَاعْفُ عَنِّى
Allahumma Innaka Afuun Tuhebbul Afuwafaafu Anni.
(O Allah, You are oft-forgiving, You love to forgive, so forgive me).

A11: Eating Start: بِسْمِ اللهِ وَعَلٰى بَرَكَةِ اللهِ
Bismillahe wala brarakatillah. ((I am taking my food) with the name of Allah and with blessings of Allah)).

A12: Eating Finish: اَلْحَمْدُ لِلّٰهِ الَّذِيْ اَطْعَمَنَا وَسَقَانَا وَجَعَلَنَا مِنَ الْمُسْلِمِيْنَ
Alhamdu lillahellazi Atwamana Wasaqana Wajaalana Minul Muslimin.
(All praise is for Allah who has fed us and made us drink and made us Muslim).

A13: Sleep Start: اَللّٰهُمَّ بِاسْمِكَ اَمُوْتُ وَاَحْيٰى
Allahumma Beismeka Amutuwahia. (O Allah! I die and live with Your name).

A14: Frightening Dream or Disturbance: اَعُوْذُ بَكَلِمَاتِ اللهِ التَّامَّةِ مِنْ غَضَبِهِ وَشَرِّ عِبَادِهِ وَمِنْ هَمَزَاتِ الشَّيَاطِيْنْ وَاَنْ يَحْضُرُوْنَ
Auzube Kalimatillahet Taammati Min Ghazabihi Waeqabihi Washarre Ebadihi Wamin Hamazatis Shayatinne Waaiyahjurun. (I invoke

perfect words of Allah for protection against His Wrath, anger and punishment and the mischief of His servants and the evil promoting of Satan and against their coming even near me).

A15: Wakeup: اَلْحَمْدُ لِلَّهِ الَّذِء أَحْيَانَا بَعْدَمَا أَمَاتَنَا وَإِلَيْهِ النُّشُوْرُ

Alhamdu Lillahellazi Ahyana Baadama Amatana Wailaihen Nushur. (All praise is for Allah who has raised us to life after having caused us to die and to Him is the (resurrection))

A16: Wearing Clothes: اللَّهُمَّ إِنِّى اَسْأَلُكَ مِنْ خَيْرِهِ وَخَيْرَ مَاهُوَلَهُ وَأَعُوْذُبِكَ مِنْ شَرِّهِ وَشَرِّمَا هُوَلَه

Allahumma Inni Asaluka Min Khairihi Wakhairihi Mahualahu Auzubeka Min Sarrihi Washarrema Hualahu. (O Allah, I ask You the goodness of this clothes and goodness of that for which it is made and I seek Your protection from the evil of this clothes and evil of that for which it can be used).

A17: Look into Mirror: اَللَّهُمَّ اَنْتَ حَسَّنْتَ خَلْقِىْ فَحَسِنْ خُلُقِىْ

Allahumma Anta Hassanta Khalqi Fahussin Khuluqi. (O Allah, You have given me good physical form so also favor me with good morals and manners.

A18: Oath Taking: وَاللهِ بِاللهِ

Wallah Billah. (Swear by Allah)

A19: Enter and Leave Home: اَللَّهُمَّ إِنِّى اَسْئَلُكَ خَيْرَ الْمَوْلِجُ وَخَيْرَا الْمَخْرَج بِسْمِ اللهِ وَلَجْنَا ويِسْم اللهِ خَرَجْنَا وَعَلَى اللهِ رِيّنَا تَوَكَّلْنَا

Allahumma Anni Asaluka Khairal Maolaji Wakhairal Makhraji Bismillahe Walajna Wabismillahe Kharajna Waalallahe Rabbena Tawakkalna. (O Allah! I beg of You the blessings of entering and leaving. With Allah's name do we enter and with Allah's name do we leave and upon Allah, our Lord, do we rely).

A20: Hearing Good News: الْحَمْدُ لِلّهِ

Alhamdulillah. (All praise be to Allah).

A21: Visit Market / Store / Mall:
When one recites this du'a in market, Allah credits him / her one million virtues, deletes one million sins, raises status by one million stages and builds a palace in Paradise.

لَا إِلَهَ إِلاَّ اللهُ وَحْدَهُ لَاشَرِيْكَ لَهُ لَهُ الْمُلْكُ وَلَهُ الْحَمْدُ يُحْيِىْ وَيُمِيْتُ بِيَدِهِ الْخَيْرُ وَهُوَ عَلَى كُلِّ شَيْءٍ قَدِيْرٌ

La Ilaha Illallahu Wahdahu Lasharikalahu Lahul Mulku Walahul Humdu Yuhee WayumituWahua Hyyun Layamutu Biyadihil Khairu Wahua Ala Kulle Shaiyen qadir. (None is worthy of worship except Allah, He is One, He has no partner, to Him belongs the sovereign and for Him is all praise, He gives life and death, He is Ever-living and never dies, in His hand is all good, and He has power over all things).

A22: Bad News: اِنَّا لِلّهِ وَاِنَّا اِلَيْهِ رَاجِعُوْن

Innalillahe Wainnailaihe Rajiun. (Surely we belong to Allah and verily to Him we return)

A23: Problem arises: تَوَكَّلْتُ عَلَى اللهَ

Tawakkalto Ala-Allah. (I put my trust in Allah)

A24: Pain and Distress: يَا الله

Ya Allah. (O Allah).

A25: Unpleasant occurs: نَعُوْذُ بِاللهِ

Nauzobillah. (We seek refuge with Allah)

A26: See Something Not Pleasing: اَلْحَمْدُ لِلّهِ كُلّ حَالٍ

Alhumdulillahe Ala Kulle Hal. (All praise be due to Allah in all conditions).

A27: Grief, Sorrow, Sick: لاَحَوْلَ وَلاَ قُوَّةَ اِلاَّ بِاللهِ

La Haulawala quwwata Illabilla. (There is no strength and power besides the strength and power of Allah).

A28: Debt or Financial Difficulty: اَللّهُمَّ اكْفِنِيْ بِحَلاَلِكَ عَنْ حَرَامِكَ وَاَغْنِنِيْ بَقَضْلِكَ عَمَّنْ سِوَاكَ

Allahummuk Finni Behalalika An Haramika Wagfini Befudlika Ammun Sewaka. (O Allah, provide me with lawful livelihood, adequate to my needs instead of ill-gotten one, and graciously grant me freedom from needing anything from anyone besides Yourself).

A29: Panic Mode / Angry: اَعُوْذُ بِاللهِ مِنَ الشَّيْطَانِ الرَّجِيْم

Auzubillahe Minash Shaitaner Rajim. (I seek refuge in Allah from the accursed devil).

A30: Feel Helpless: حِسْبِيَ اللهُ وَنِعْمَ الْوَكِيْلُ

Hasbenallahu Waneemalwakil. (Allah is sufficient for me and what an excellent Patron He is).

A31: Pain in Body: اَعُوْذُ بِاللهِ وَقُدْرَتِه مِنْ شَرِّ مَاَاجِدُ وَاُحَاذِرُ

Auzubillahe Waqudratihi Minsharrema Ajidu Wa Uhazeru.
(I seek refuge in Allah and His power against the mischief of that pain which I feel and fear).

A32: Treatment of Wound: يُشْفَى سَقِيْمُنَا بِاذْنِ رَبِّنَا
Yushfa Saqimuna Biizni Rabbina. (Our sick man should become well with the will of our Lord).

A33: Sick Person Recites: لَاإِلَهَ إِلاَّ اَنْتَ سُبْحَانَكَ اِنِّى كُنْتُ مِنَ الظَّالِمِيْنَ
La Ilaha Illa Anta Subhanaka Inni Kuntu Minazzlimin. (There is none worthy of worship except You. All purity belongs to You. Surely I am from among the wrongdoers).

A34: Repentance: اَللّهُمَّ اِنِّىْ اَتُوْبُ اِلَيْكَ مِنْهَا لاَاَرْجِعُ اِلَيْهَا اَبَدًا
Allahumma Inni Atubu Ilaika Minha La Arjeu Ilaiha Abadun.
(O Allah, I repent before You for all my sins and I promise never to return to the same (again)).

A35: Death Time: اَللّهُمَّ اغْفِرْلِىْ وَارْحَمْنِىْ وَاَلْحِقْنِىْ بِالرَّفِيْقِ الْاَعْلَى
Allahummaghfirli Waarhamni Walhequni Berrafiqel Aala.
(O Allah, forgive me, have mercy on me and unite me with the Most High Companion).

B1: Greet a Muslim: اَلسَّلاَمُ عَلَيْكُمْ وَرَحْمَةُ اللهِ وَبَرَكَاتُه
Assalamu Alaikum Warahmatullahe Wabrarakatuhu.
(May the peace of Allah descend upon you and His mercy and blessings)

B2: Salam Reply: وَعَلَيْكُمُ السَّلاَمُ وَرَحْمَةُ اللهِ وَبَرَكَاتُه
Waalaikumus Salam Warahmatullahe Wabarakatuhu. (And upon you (also) be the peace of Allah, His mercy and blessings).

B3: See a Muslim Happy: اَضْحَكَ اللهُ سِنَّكَ
Azhakallahu Sinnaka. (May Allah keep you happy and laughing forever).

B4: Befriend a Muslim: اِنِّى اُحِبُّكَ فِىْ اللهِ
Inni Uhebbuka Fillah. (I love you for the sake of Allah).

B5: Greet any Non-Muslim: عَلَيْكُمْ or عَلَيْكَ
Alaika or Alaikum. (Upon you)

B6: Reply any Non-Muslim: وَعَلَيْكُمْ or وَعَلَيْكَ
Waalaika or Waalaikum. (And upon you, too).

B7: Express Appreciation: مَاشَاءَ الله
Masaallah. (What Allah has willed)

B8: Thank Someone: جَزَاكَ اللهُ خَيْرًا
Jazakallahu Khaira. (May Allah Reward you well).

B9: When Sneeze: اَلْحَمْدُ لِلَّهِ
Alhumdulillah. (Thanks and all praise be to Allah).

B10: Reply to one who Sneezes: يَرْحَمُكَ اللهِ
Yarhamukallah. (May Allah have mercy on you).

B11: Visit a Sick: اللّهُمَّ اشْفِهِ اَللّهُمَّ عَافِهِ
Allahummashfihi Allahummaafihi. (O Allah, cure him and make him well).

B12: Parting Someone: فِىْ اَمَانِ اللهِ
Fiaman Allah. (In Allah's Trust)

B13: Bidding Farewell: اَسْتَوْدِعُ اللهَ دِيْنَكَ وَاَمَانَتَكَ وَخَوَاتِيْمَ عَمَلِكَ
Astaodew Allah Dinaka Waamanataka Wakhawateema Amaleka. (I give in trust to Allah your religion, your belongings and the result of your deeds).

C1: Give Charity: فِىْ سَبِيْلِ اللهِ
Fisabilillah. (in the path of Allah)

C2: Masjid In: اَللّهُمَّ اقْتَحْ لِىْ أَبْوَابَ رَحْمَتِكَ
Allahumaftahli Abwaba Rahmatek. (O Allah! Open the doors of Your Mercy).

C3: Masjid Out: اَللّهُمَّ إِنِّى أَسْألُكَ مِنْ فَضْلِكَ
Allahumma Inni Asaluka Min Fadlik. (O Allah! I beg of You Your favor)

C4: Mashwara / Consultation: اَللّهُمَّ اَلْهِمْنَا مَرَاشِرَ أُمُوْرِنَا وَنَعُوْذُبِكَ مِنْ شُرُوْرِ اَنْفُسِنَا وَمِنْ سَيِّئَاتِ أَعَمَالِنَا
Allahumma Alhemna Marasheda Umurena Wa-naozubeka Minshuruea Anfusena Wamin Sayyeate Amalena.
(O Allah! Inspire us with your guidance in our needs, we seek refuge in you from the evils of our souls and punishment of our bad deed).

C5: Bayan / Speech Start: رَبِّ اشْرَحْ لِىْ صَدْرِىْ وَيَسِّرْلِىْ اَمْرِىْ وَاحْلُلْ عُقْدَةَ مِّنْ لِسَانِى يَفْقَهُوْا قَوْلِىْ رَبِّ زِدْنِىْ عِلْمًا

Rabbesrahle Sadre Wayassarli Amri Waahlul Okdatum Mallasani Yafkahu Kaoli Rabbi Zedni Elmun.

(O my Lord! Enlighten my chest and make my task easy and open a knot of my tongue that they may understand my speech. O my Lord! Increase my knowledge).

C6: Talim / Bayan / Speech Finish: سُبْحَانَكَ اللَّهُمَّ وَبِحَمْدِكَ اَشْهَدُ اَنْ لاَّاِلَهَ اِلاَّ اَنْتَ اَسْتَغْفِرُكَ وَاَتُوْبُ اِلَيْكَ

Subhanaka Allahumma Wabehamdika Ashadu Allahilaha Illaanta Wastagferuka Watubuilai.

Glory be to You, praise be to You O Allah! We bear witness that there is no one worthy of worship but You, we repent to You and we ask You for forgiveness and we repent to You).

D1: Journey: بِسْمِ اللهِ تَوَكَّلْتُ عَلَى اللهِ لاَحَوْلَ وَلاَ قُوَّةَ اِلاَّ بِاللهِ

Bismillahe Tawakkaltu Alallahe Lahaolawala Kuwata Illabillah.

(In the name of Allah, I rely upon Allah. There is no might and no power, except with Allah)

اَللَّهُمَّ بِكَ اَصُوْلُ وَبِكَ اَحُوْلُ وَبِكَ اَسِيْرُ

Allahumma Bika Adullu Wabeka Ahulu Wabeka Asiru. (O Allah, with Your help I attack and with Your help I plan and plot and with Your help I undertake this journey).

D2: Car / Plane: سُبْحَانَ الَّذِى سَخَّرَلَنَا هَذَا وَمَا كُنَّالَهُ مُقْرِنِيْنَ وَاِنَّا اِلَى رَبِّنَا لَمُنْقَلِبُوْنَ

Sobhanallaji Sakharalana Haja Wama Kunnalahu Mukrinin Wainnaila Rabbana Lamunkalebun.

(Glorified is He who subjugated this for us, otherwise we could not bring it into subjugation. And surely, we are to return to our Lord).

D3: Ship: بِسْمِ اللهِ مَجْرِهَا وَمُرْسِهَا اِنَّ رَبِّىْ لَغَفُوْرٌ رَّحِيْمُ

Bismillahe Majriha Wamursaha Innarabbi Lagafurur Rahim.

(With the name of Allah is its course and its mooring. Indeed, my Lord is Forgiving, Merciful).

D4: Enter City: اَللَّهُمَّ بَارِكْ لَنَا فِيْهَا

Allahumma Bareklana Fiha (O Allah! You grant us good in it).

Different Etiquette

Qur'an Recitation Etiquette

1. Every Muslim must learn, understand, and live by the Qur'an. Whoever learns the Qur'an and teaches it is the best amongst us. It removes the rust on the heart and guides to success. The person who is blessed with the Qur'anic knowledge got the best blessing.

2. The person who memorized the Qur'an and acted accordingly will be able to take 10 sinful people among his / her relatives from Hell to Paradise by Allah's order. The person that has difficulty reading Qur'an yet tries his / her best to learn it will get double the reward than a fluent reader.

3. The best time to read Qur'an is in the early morning. Make Wudu and say *Auzubillahe Minas Saitaner Rajim* and *Bismillaher Rahmaner Rahim* before reciting the Qur'an.

4. Try your best to learn the rules of recitation so you can pronounce everything correctly and distinctly. Allah eagerly loves to listen to the person who recites the Qur'an.

5. Be attentive when you recite the Qur'an and when others recite. You get 10 rewards for each letter you recite in the Qur'an.

6. Make sejda when you see a prostration mark in the Qur'an.

7. When reading about punishment or sins, be fearful and seek refuge to Allah. When reading about rewards and paradise, say *Subhanallah* and ask Allah to grant you that happiness.

8. Remember that these are the words of Allah, and you must take care of the Qur'an respectfully.

9. Don't slam the Qur'an here and there, or put something on top of it like you handle ordinary books.

10. After reciting Qur'an, say *Sadaqallahul Aaleyul Aazem* (The most High, the Mighty Allah spoke the truth). We should thank Allah for sending this Qur'an for our guidance.

11. If you want to be a good Muslim, you should see how Muhammad (ﷺ) and his companions followed the Qur'an, and follow them in order to act Islamically.

Masjid Etiquette

1. When you go into a Masjid, be sure your clothes are clean and you have Wudu.
2. Enter with your right foot first saying *Assalamualaykum* and *Allahumaftahle Abwaba Rahmathek* (O Allah, open the doors of your mercy).
3. Make two rakats of Nafl Salat to greet the Masjid.
4. Don't talk idle or haram things like gossip or disturb others. Your intention should be to worship Allah.
5. Keep the Masjid clean. Whoever builds a Masjid for Allah, Allah builds a house for him / her in paradise.
6. Leave the Masjid with the left foot out first and say *Allahumma Inne Asaloka Min fadhlek* (O Allah, I ask You of Your bounty).

When a Child is Born

1. Give thanks to Allah (ﷻ), examples: say *Alhamdulillah*, Make Salah as gratitude to Allah, give some money or food to needy as charity, etc.
2. Give Azan to the ears of the child.
3. Say *Bismillah* and let the child lick the fingertip with honey or chewed dates (very small amounts).
4. Give a good name relating to names of Allah or name of a Sahaba.
5. On the 7th day, sacrifice 2 goat or sheep for a boy and 1 for a girl. It is sadaqa for the child's life. Shave the hair of the newborn. If possible weigh the hair and give the amount of silver in charity to the poor. You may have an Aquiqa and invite people to dinner but avoid extravaganza.
6. Circumcise for boy.
7. Child's rights:
   a. Get a pious Muslim mother, so she can train the child from childhood to be pious.
   b. Get a nice name.
   c. Feed mother's milk for 30 months of the child's birth (If possible).
   d. To get Islamic education, bring him / her to an Islamic community, play with Muslim children, teach the value of Qur'anic teachings, teach how to do good and stop evil, feed halal earned, halal food, teach about kindness and simple lifestyles.

Muslim Dress

1. Wear neat, clean and simple dress that does not show pride, vanity, or arrogance. Allah dislikes all arrogant people.
2. Don't buy dresses or shoes more than you need. For Allah doesn't like wasters. Waster's are like the brother of Satan.
3. Men don't wear silk, bright red, bright yellow garments, nor they are permitted to wear gold but women are permitted.
4. Men don't cover their ankles but women do.
5. Women should not wear tight, thin dress that exposes their body features / shapes. They should properly cover themselves in public. (Surah An-Noor).
6. Men should not dress like women nor should women dress like men. If they do, Allah will curse them.
7. Don't wear clothes with photographs of animal or people.
8. Prophets used to wear turbine and cap.
9. Wear the dress (and shoe) with the right side first saying *bismillah* and thank Allah for the dress. Wear your best and clean clothes for Salat especially on Juma day.
10. While taking off clothes or shoes, start from your left side.
11. When you see yourself in the mirror, say: *Allahumma Hassanta Khalkee Fahassen Khoolookee.* (Oh Allah, you created me so beautiful, so make my character also beautiful).
12. Don't wear clothes that symbolize other religions.
13. Don't wear old torn clothes, but you are encouraged to wear clothes that are not too old. It is said that wearing old clothes is part of faith.

Etiquette of Eating and Drinking

1. Allah does not accept good deeds if food is not halal (which is defined legal by Qur'an).
2. Avoid eating or drinking haram (which is defined illegal by Qur'an) such as: blood, alcohol, lottery, pork, animal meat which is not slaughtered in the name of Allah, food sacrificed or donated in the name of saints, even the Prophet (ﷺ).
3. Food or drink obtained from illegal funds is haram such as: unjustly taken property or money of someone or orphans, bribery, cheating, theft, interest, gambling, and profits from business encouraging disobedience to Allah.
4. Avoid eating doubtful things.

5. Wash both hands up to wrist and small mouth rinse with water.
6. Sit on both feet (best position) or like sitting during Salat or one leg up and sit on other leg.
7. When you see the food which is being served, say: *Allahumma Bariklana Fema Razaqtana Waqina Azabannar* (O Allah bestow blessings for us in what You have provided us and save us from the punishment of the Fire).
8. Before eating, say: *Bismillah Wala Barakatilla* (in the name of Allah and on the blessings of Allah). Mention the name of Allah before eating or Satan shares meal, but if one forgets to say it at the beginning, then when he / she remembers, should say: *Bismillahi Awaluhu Waakhira* (in the name of Allah in the beginning and end).
9. Eat with the right hand because Satan eats with his left. You get more blessing if you share your food.
10. Eat what is closest to you on your plate. If food falls, clean it and eat it.
11. Don't say bad things about food, if you don't like it, avoid it.
12. Do not eat hot or burned food.
13. Don't overeat. Eat 1/3rd full with food, 1/3rd with water, leave 1/3rd for zikr.
14. Do not eat or drink from gold or silver dishes or utensils.
15. When drinking water, use right hand to hold or touch glass, take 3 pauses saying *Bismillah* before and *Alhamdulilla* after.
16. Clean your plate and lick your fingers.
17. When finished eating: say *Alhamdu Lillahillaze Atamana Wasaqanaa Wajaalna Minal Muslimen* (All praise is to Allah who fed us and provided us drink and made us Muslims).
18. ZamZam water may be drunk standing and facing the Qibla and making du'a.
19. When you thank Allah after eating, He is pleased and gives the reward of fasting.

Sitting

1. Do not take someone else's seat.
2. Do not separate two people who are sitting together or cause them to stop talking.
3. Do not move your head frequently as it will disturb view from back.

4. If someone sneezes, he / she should say *Alhamdulilla*, and the others should answer *Yarhamukalla*.
5. If you yawn, cover your mouth and say: *La Howla Wala Quwwata Illabilla* (There is no movement or power besides with Allah)

Consultation / Mashwara

1. It is Sunnah of Rasul (ﷺ). He used to consult with his companions on issues.
2. Amir or faisal decides on the final decision.
3. Recite du'a of Mashwara.
4. Faisal asks opinion from everyone or whomever he chooses.
5. Opinion is a trust and should be short and to the point, not a long lecture supporting your opinion.
6. No one should cut others opinion but if your opinion is contrary to another, just say your opinion, don't compare your opinion against others.
7. Amir makes final decision. All those whose opinions are not accepted should thank Allah, one whose opinion is accepted should be afraid of its shortcomings and consequences
8. All should agree in the final decision of Faisal as your opinion.

Talking

1. Talk in a polite and moderate voice, don't shout or talk in an extremely high or rude voice because Allah does not like it. Invite people to Islam with wisdom and beautiful preaching. We should not abuse what other people worship. Don't quarrel about religion, don't force people, because truth is clear.
2. Remember that the person who invites people to do good deeds is given the same rewards, which people do as the result of his invitation. Allah hates a person when he says other people to do good but himself does not.
3. Don't use bad language like ridiculing each other, mock, call names, spy on each other, insult, taunt, backbite, for backbiting is like eating the flesh of your dead brother and is punished in the grave, don't curse, don't blame a person without any fault, or blaming a person for your own fault, stay away from useless talk, swear or say anything that causes fight or division of people (read Surah Hujurat).
4. Speak the truth, be an honest witness, stand out for justice, even though it is against your own relatives.

5. Say *Inshallah* (Allah willing) when saying I will do something in the future. If you see something wonderful in Allah's creation, Say *Rabbanah ma Khalaqtha Haza Batelan Subhanaka Faquenah Aazabannar* (Oh lord, you didn't create anything in vain, you are free from all faults, and save us from your hell fire) You will be counted as a good person or knowledgeable person. You can also praise Allah by saying *Subhanalla Alhumdulilla* etc.

6. Don't brag about yourself for Allah doesn't like the proud. Allah gives his Deen to the humble souls. Never get extremely angry, controlling anger is a virtue.

7. Listen to other people respectfully, don't interrupt the speech. You may ask questions later. Don't stay away from common people, ignore their faults, and set a good example among them. Teach them about Islam. Avoid stubborn arrogant people politely by saying Salam.

8. Talk to your youngster with affection and to your elders and knowledgeable persons with respect.

9. Many people will be thrown into Hell because of the sayings of their tongue. Whosoever believes in Allah and the Last Day either speaks well or keeps silent. Keep your hands and mouth from harming another Muslim or a neighbor.

10. If you have nothing to say, keep your tongue moist with Allah's remembrance. You will be victorious before Allah. *Saying Subhan Allahe Wabeham Dehe Subhan Allahil Azem* (Allah is free from all faults, and I am praising Him, and He is the Most Perfect, the Magnificent). It is heavy in the reward's scale, but light in your tongue. Anyone remembers Allah, Allah remembers him.

Walking

1. Walk in a humble manner because Allah does not like pride. Do not push each other in order to get ahead of other people.

2. Keep your eyesight down and away from unlawful objects such as bad pictures on billboards, not properly dressed men and women, etc.

3. Removing obstacles from the path is part of Iman, in case people get hurt or stumble (informing people of broken bridges, railway paths, holes in the streets, etc).

4. Man should not walk together with non-mahram women and the same for women also.

5. Women should not go out in public with strong perfume or make trickling noises with her ornaments to attract attention to herself. She should properly cover her body. Man should modestly cover himself.

Journeys and Visits

1. Be prepared for the long journey with enough money, food, clothes, proper documents.
2. Before leaving the house, say *Bismillaahi Tawakkaltu Alaallaah* (in the name of Allah, I put my trust on Allah) and *La Hawlaa Wala Quwwata Illaabillaahil Aliyyul Adheem* then he is guided, cared for, and protected by Allah *Subhana Wata'aala.*
3. When using transportation, say: *Alhamdulillaahi Subhanallazi Sakharalana Haza Wama Kunna Lahu Muqrinen Wainna Ilarabbina Lamunqalibon* (All praise is for Allah, glory be to Allah who controlled this for us though we were not able to control it and we will surely return to our lord).
4. When crossing a bridge or travel by ship: *say, Bismillahe Majreha Wamursaha Innarabbila Gafurur Rahim.* (With the name of Allah is its course and its mooring. Indeed my lord is forgiving, and merciful).
5. Take care of Fellow Traveler.
6. When entering a city pray to Allah for your safe stay and return
7. When entering your home say bismillaah and salaam then Satan cannot enter the house. Thank Allah for bringing you back safely.
8. Ask permission when entering other people's house. If permission is not given then leave saying salaam respectfully.
9. Don't give salam to non-Muslim's but you can say *wa'alaikum.*
10. Shake hands with Muslims of the same gender when giving salaam.
11. Allah's love is due to those who love each other, sit with each other, visit one another and spend on each other for Allah's sake.
12. Visit and care for the sick, even if you can only offer them kind words. Whoever visits a sick person for Allah's sake angels pray for him / her saying: may you be well, may your passage be well, and may you occupy a place in paradise.
13. Sickness cleanses a person's sins.
14. If you pray for a person in his absence, angels pray for you saying *"same for you also".*

Bathroom

1. Before you enter the toilet say: *Auzoo Billah Himeenal Khobosee Walkhabais* (Oh Allah! I seek refuge in you from the devil and all kinds of evils).
2. Cover head inside bathroom.
3. Do not recite Qur'an, Hadith or make zikr.
4. Do not talk inside.
5. Do not use toilet facing Qibla.
6. Wipe before you sit, best way to sit is squat.
7. Place tissue paper in water of toilet so that water does not splash back to you.
8. While urinating, take extra caution not to splash urine on yourself. Do not urinate while standing. Hold tissue paper after you urinate at the tip (for male) and walk and cough to ensure no additional urine drop is coming from inside.
9. After using toilet, use left hand to wipe with tissue paper, clean up sitting area, flush toilet for next person.
10. When you come out: put your right foot out first, and say: *Ghufranaka Alhamdulilla hillaze Azhaba Anil Aza Wa Afane*. (I seek your pardon, all praises are due to Allah who has taken away from me discomfort and granted me relief).

Sleeping

1. Go to sleep as soon as possible after Isa prayer, preferably with Wudu.
2. Read Sura Ikhlas, Falaq, and Nas 3 times each, Ayatul Kurse.
3. Say *Subhanalla* 33 times, *Alhamdulillal* 33 times, *Allahuakbar* 34 times.
4. Do not lie down or sleep on your stomach. It is sunnah to use oil on head and kohl in eyes.
5. While sleeping, face Qibla on your right side. Keep right hand under the cheek.
6. Before sleeping say: *Allaahumma Bismika Amootoo Wahya* (O Allah in your name I die and live).
7. Try to wake up for Tahajjud, and if you sincerely try but miss it, you will still be rewarded for your intentions. Getting up to make Tahajjud Salat in the later part of night is a sign of great piousness.
8. Good dreams are from Allah and bad dreams are from Satan. If you see a bad dream, then say *La Howla Wala Quwwata Illabilla*

and *Auzubillahe Minas Saitaner Rajim*, spit lightly 3 times over your left shoulder, and don't tell anyone.

9. When waking up, say: *Alhamdulillahillaji Ahyana Bada Mamatana Wailaihin Nusor* (All praise is for Allah who revived us after our death and to Him will be our raising on the Day of Judgment).

10. Make Wudu, preferably with meswak (Wudu with meswak makes Salat 70 times more valuable than without meswak).

11. Make Salat, glorify Allah and read Qur'an because angels witness at that time.

Dealing with Others
Parents and Family

1. Behave nicely with your parents; in their old age, take care of them no matter how difficult it is, do not even say "oof" to them. A glance at your parent with affection will give you reward of an accepted Hajj.

2. Talk politely, respectfully with them. Do not get upset with them. Whoever takes good care of his parents, Allah will increase his life-span with His blessings. Pray for your parents by saying: *Rabbir Hamhuma Kama Rabba Yane Saghera.* (Oh Lord! Have mercy on them the way they used to be merciful to us in our infancy).

3. Always obey them if they do not go against Islam. Be helpful to them by doing housework for them. Help them raise younger siblings. Don't be too demanding beyond their capacity. Show appreciation when they do good things for you. Overlook their faults. Use kind words when you try to correct them.

4. In case one's parents are not Muslim or un-Islamic, you should still care for them, respect them, and obey them unless they order you to disobey Allah; try to encourage them to Islam kindly and gently and with the wisdom of Qur'an.

5. Your parents' rights over you are: you make sure they do not go hungry and have clothes and a place to live; take care of them in their sickness according to your capacity.

6. In case they are dead, ask for forgiveness for Muslim parents. Try to pay off their debts. Be kind to their loved ones.

7. Grandparents, uncles, and aunts on both mother's and father's sides have similar rights.

8. Remember that the money you spend on your family earns the most reward from Allah.
9. Never break blood relations. If you do, you will be forbidden to enter Paradise.
10. If you take an oath, which is causing hardship to your family, you must break it and pay recompense for breaking the oath.

Business Dealings

1. Earn lawful livelihood. Allah will not accept good deeds with earnings from haram sources.
2. Keep balance in your trade with truth and honesty. Don't give less in measure when dealing with people. Cheaters will be in grave destruction.
3. Have extra kindness when dealing with a poor person, so that Allah will be kind to you on the Day of Judgment.
4. Do not swear frequently to promote your merchandise.
5. When lending money to people, take written agreements and 2 witnesses.
6. A person must make a **Will** of his / her belongings Islamically.

Spouse

1. When marrying, choose a pious partner.
2. The marriage is not valid unless both people agree to get married and are not forced into it.
3. The couple should love one another and never be cruel or mean to each other.
4. Allah says husbands and wives are a comfort for each other and try to be most kind to one another. Husbands must not be tyrants, but rather a just and kind ruler of the house. Similarly, wives should not be stubborn and insensitive to her husband unless it is a violation of Allah's law.
5. Husband and wife should respect each other, consult one another, and they should not let the Satan come between them. The Satan is happiest when he has divided husband and wife.
6. They should give each other their rights and help each other to do good. They should take proper responsibility for their families and children in providing for them, loving them, and bringing them up Islamically.

7. They should trust each other and depend on Allah. Believing men and women will each get their full rewards from Allah and Allah values both of them.
8. When they have problems they should try to achieve peace through understanding and kindness.

Neighbors and others (including animals)

1. Greet Muslims with salaam and handshake by saying *Yagfirullahu Lana walakum*, may Allah forgive you and me. It erases sins and takes away hatred. Be a helpful neighbor. Don't bother them. Help them if they are needy with money and Islamic knowledge. Non-Muslims have the right to be informed of Islam.
2. If they are sick, visit them, help them; in their troubled times console them. Help them every way you can. Never take anyone's thing without asking permission.(whether in your family or neighbors)
3. Take special care of orphans and widows whether they are your relatives or neighbors. Same for sick people, whether in your family or neighbors.
4. Help travelers giving them water, shelter, or directions.
5. Be generous and kind to your guests.
6. Be very kind to Allah's creatures. Whoever doesn't show kindness to Allah's creatures does not deserve kindness from Allah (a lady was thrown in Hellfire because she tortured a cat; another person was guided to right path and granted Jannah because he was kind to a thirsty dog).
7. If you have to kill an animal, make it quick and do not let it suffer; when sacrificing an animal, be sure the knife is sharp.
8. If a Muslim presents an excuse, accept it. Do not be critical about it. If he asks for forgiveness for his faults, forgive him for Allah's sake and Allah will forgive your faults. Hide a Muslim's faults, Allah will hide your faults.
9. Feel deep concern for his loss and be happy for his gain. If you remove one difficulty from someone, Allah will remove one difficulty in the Day of Judgment.
10. Whoever is not respectful to the elders and kind to the young, are not good Muslims.
11. Be grateful if someone helps you and let him know that by saying: *Jazaakallaahu Bilkhair* (May Allah reward you with the good).

12. In extreme cases don't hold grudges against each other for more than three days or both parties' good deeds will not be accepted by Allah.
13. Make peace between two quarreling parties. Don't be the mischief-makers on Allah's earth.
14. A Muslim wants for other Muslims what he or she wants for him or herself.
15. Call and remind each other constantly to obey Allah, and discourage each other from evil things and rush to do good!

Some Good and Bad Qualities

1. Fear Allah because His punishment is the worst.
2. Be sincere in all of your actions. Allah does not accept any deed that is not done for Him only. If you do any good deed for Allah, no matter how small it is, He will reward you generously. A martyr was thrown in Hell because he was fighting to get famous, and not to please Allah.
3. Fear Allah whether your deeds are acceptable or not to Him. If you did some good deed for someone, don't even mention it in a manner so you could make him feel bad. Then that good deed will be destroyed.
4. Be thankful to Allah. He will increase His blessings on you (Including your ability to do good). No matter how much we thank Him, it's not enough compared to the blessings we get from Him. Allah is so generous, and decent, that He highly appreciates when we thank Him. Ungratefulness to Allah will cause you to lose His blessings.
5. Never break just promises. Always stand up for justice even if it is against your parents.
6. Be punctual, and don't delay to do any good deed if you already intended to do it because you may never have another chance.
7. Stay away from luxury and don't be a miser, either. Be moderate in your lifestyle. Adopt a simple lifestyle. Don't be wasteful because wasters are the brothers of Satan. Sit with the people who remember Allah in the morning and in the evening seeking only Allah's pleasure. Don't overlook those people.
8. Stay away from bad company. Do not sit with the people who make fun of Allah's rules, unless they change the subject.
9. Don't be angry because it is from Satan. Say *Auzobillah*
10. and ask Allah's help to control your anger. If you control your

temper, Allah will save you from His anger on the Day of Judgment.

11. Seek Allah's help in your trouble time with patience and Salat. Allah is with the patience, and Allah alone is enough for your protector and guide. When trouble happens, say *Inna Lillahe Wainna Ilaihe Rajeun* (Surely we all belong to Allah and surely we will all return to him).

12. Don't be envious of each other because envy eats up goodness as fire eats up fuel.

13. Don't beg because Allah likes the one who works for his / her livelihood.

14. Don't believe in fortune telling, it will destroy all your good deed. Because believing in fortune telling is Shirk. Also don't eat haram food. If you do your prayers will not be accepted for forty days.

15. Don't make groups in Allah's Deen. Allah is one, and Islam is His chosen religion for us. Stay as close to Qur'an and sunnah teachings as close as possible.

16. Don't invent new things in religion that will take you to hell or deny anything from Allah's Deen.

17. Don't create hardship in religion. Forgive each other so you can get Allah's forgiveness. Hold fast to Allah's Deen all together.

18. Hold fast to the rope of Allah and do not be disunited.

19. Allah is knowledgeable. He likes to see that we have knowledge. It is compulsory to learn Islamic knowledge for both men and women. Traveling to earn Islamic knowledge is like in the jihad until he returns, and while he is away, angels, all the animals, fish, even ants in their hole, pray for him.

20. The first word from Allah is "**Read**". Please read the Qur'an with the meaning. Whose talk can be better than Allah's? His given knowledge is the best. Learn how to be successful through Qur'an. When a nation disobeys Allah, He destroys them and creates a new nation. Such a nation who loves Allah, and Allah loves them. Why don't we be that special nation to Allah? If you want to learn about Paradise and Hell, and Allah's wonderful signs, read especially Surah Yasin, Ar-Rahman, Al-Waqi'ah, Al-Mulq, etc.

Some Good Deeds

1. If you say Durud (*Allahumma Salleala Muhammadur Rasulullah*) one time, Allah will give you 10 blessings, 10 rewards, and forgive 10 sins.
2. Saying *Subhanallah* (Allah is far away from any defect) 100 times will erase 1000 sins or add 1000 rewards on our deed book.
3. Reading or teaching 1 verse from the Qur'an early in the morning will give you the reward of as if you donated 1 camel among the poor people. However many verses you read will equal that many camels.
4. 5 times Salats will wash your sins off as if you take a bath 5 times a day in river water.
5. Doing meswak before Salah will increase your Salah by 70 times.
6. There are 360 joints in our body. Every day we must pay 1 sadqa for each joint. 2 rakat of Salatul Duha will be sufficient for that. (Saying 1 *subhanallah*, 1 *alhamdulillah*, 1 *Allahakbar*, helping someone, removing something harmful from the street etc. are each valued as 1 sadqa.)
7. Saying Surah Ikhlas, Falaq, and Nas 3 times each in the morning and evening will give you protection from every harmful thing.
8. If you visit a sick person 70,000 angels pray for your forgiveness.
9. *La Howla wa la koo wata illa billa hil aleeyool azeem* (there is no power nor might except from Allah, the magnificent) is a sentence from the treasure of paradise. This has a cure for 99 diseases, the least of them is your worry.
10. Praying Isha Salat in congregation is as if you prayed until midnight and praying Fajr Salat in congregation is as if you prayed from midnight until morning. So if you pray these two Salah, you will have the rewards of whole night prayer.
11. Anyone praying for his brother in his absence, angels pray for him by saying "*the same be for you too*".
12. If you say: *Sayidul Istegfar* one time in the morning and evening, and if you die in the night or day, you will go to Paradise.
13. Saying last two ayats of Baqara once in the evening will suffice for you for whole night.
14. By saying subhanallah and alhamdulillah and allahu akbar 33 times each after every Salat, the poor can get the same reward as rich people get by spending their wealth to perform pilgrimage, Umrah, jihad, and charity.

15. If you maintain to say *Subhanallah, Alhamdulillah, Allahuakbar* 10 times each after each Salah and before going to bed say 33 times *Subhanallah, Alhamdulillah*, and 34 times *Allahuakbar*, then you would enter Paradise. It's easy, but few do it.

16. Now you see how easy it is to get so much rewards by doing so little. How can we get it? If it is not given by Allah. The Prophet said that he is just a messenger, but the grant is from Allah. One day he advised his beloved companion Mu'ath, holding his hand: O Mu'ath, by Allah, I love you. So make sure you never give up saying *Allahumma Ainne Alazhikrika Washukrika Wahusni Ibadatika* (O Allah help me in establishing Your remembrance, thanking You, and worshipping You properly) after every Salat.

17. If you say *La Ilaha Illallaahu Wahdahu La Sharika Lahu Lahulmulku Walahul Hamdu Wahuwa Alakulli Shayin Qadeer* 10 times will give you the reward of freeing four slaves from the progeny of Ishmael (alaihissalam).

18. When a group of people gathers together at one place to learn Allah's Deen, they will not leave without getting Allah's mercy and forgiveness.

Some Bad Deeds

1. Not believing in Allah, or joining partners with Him.(no good deeds will be accepted by Allah from them)
2. Killing someone without Islamic cause.
3. Disobeying parents if they are asking you to do something Islamic.
4. Backbiting, slandering, blaming unjustly, lying, cheating etc.
5. Not keeping clothes or body clean while urinating. (big punished in the grave because of this.)
6. Taking orphan's property, stealing, associating with interest, neglecting Salah, and being cruel and naughty or arrogant.
7. Knowingly denying any of Allah's rules.
8. Eating haram or doubtful food makes your prayer unacceptable to Allah.
9. Giving unlawfully earned money to charity is not acceptable by Allah.
10. To commit suicide is a major sin.
11. Don't be hypocrites for they will be in the lowest part of Hell. Signs of hypocrites are (a) When he speaks, he tells a lie, (b) He always breaks his promise, (c) He breaks his trusts, (d) Whenever he quarrels, he quarrels very violently in an insulting manner.

12. Don't borrow money with the intention of not paying it back.
13. Unfortunately, many Muslims unknowingly get involved in unislamic activities. If one finds that he / she is involved in this situation, don't get frustrated, immediately acknowledge that it's not right and sincerely repent to Allah. If possible, get out of the situation immediately. If you can't, at least keep hope in your heart that one day, you will get out of the situation with Allah's help. Remember that Allah loves the one who turns to Him and trusts His mercy. It is a major sin to give up hope on Allah's mercy.

Some Fortunate People

1. Seven persons who will be underneath the shade of Allah on the Day of Judgment: (a) A just ruler (b) A young man who was brought up in the worship of Allah from his childhood. (c) A man who's heart is attached to the mosque. (d) Two persons who love and meet for Allah's love and part for Allah's cause only. (e) A man who was invited by a charming noble lady to do adultery, but the man refused her invitation by saying, I am afraid of Allah. (f) A person who gives to charity so secretly that his left hand does not know what his right hand has given (g) A person who remembers Allah in seclusion and his eyes become flooded with tears. (Can you find any that suites you?)
2. Always be quick in paying back your debt.
3. If you make someone to work for you, then after he finishes his work, pay his due before his sweat dries out and before he even asks for it.

Repentance

1. Allah will forget our faults when we make them by mistake, by forgetfulness, or in the oppressed times.
2. When we make mistakes, we should make sincere repentance. Allah loves those who repent sincerely, he washes their sins and exchanges them with virtues.
3. The best of the sinners are the ones who repent often and try to make up for their mistakes by doing good deeds.
4. Make sure you repent before your death approaches and you are no longer able to repent because it will not be accepted.
5. Rasulullah (ﷺ) used to repent over 70 times daily.

References

1. *Taleemul Haq*, Sabbir Ahmed E. Desai, Dawatul Haq, P. O. Box 158, Umzinto, South Africa.
2. *Bashishti Zewar*, Maulana Ashraf Ali Thanvi, Kazi Publications, Lahore, Pakistan.
3. *The Noble Qur'an*, Dr. Muhammad Taqiuddin Al-Hillali, Dr. Muhammad Muhsin Khan, Darussalam, Riyadh, Saudi Arabia.
4. *Fortification of the Muslim through remembrance and Supplication from the Qur'an and the Sunnah*, Saeed Ibn Ali Ibn Wahf Al-Qahtaani, King Fahad National Library Catalog, 1996.
5. *Fazail-e-Amal*, Shaikhul Hadith Maulana Muhammad Zakariyyah Kandhalvi.
6. *Du'a Organizer*, Abdul Hye, P.O. Box 890071, Houston, TX 77289
7. *Mosnun Du'as*, Maulana Muhammad Ashek Elahi, Kutub Khana, Lahore, Pakistan.
8. *Everyday Fiqh,* Muhammad Yusuf Eslahi–Islamic Publications, Lahore, Pakistan, 1994.
9. *Authentic Supplications of the Prophet*, Waleed K.S. Al-Essa, The Daar of Islamic Knowledge, Miami, Florida, 1993.
10. *Al-Hisaul Hasin*, Allamah Muhammad Al-Jazri, Darul Ishaat, Karachi, Pakistan, 1993.
11. *Taleem-ul-Islam*, Maulana Mufti Muhammad Kefayatullah, Siddiqi Trust, Karachi, Pakistan.
12. *The 99 Beautiful Names of Allah*, Maulana M. Rafeeq Harthurani, Iqra Printers, Stanger, South Africa.
13. *Abundance of Mercy*, Maulana Muhammad Abdullah Darkhwasti, Madrasah Arabia Islamia, Azadville, South Africa.
14. *Hajj and Umrah Organizer*, Abdul Hye, P.O. Box-890071, Houston, TX 77289
15. *Hajj and Umrah*, From A To Z, Mamdouh N. Mohamed
16. *Hajj, Umrah and Ziyarah*, Sheikh Abdul-Aziz bin Abdullah bin Baz, Darussalam, Riyadh, Saudi Arabia.
17. *Virtues of Charity and Hajj*, Shaikhul Hadith Maulana Muhammad Zakariyyah Kandhalvi.
18. *The Pilgrimage*, Hajji Zakaria Kamdar, A Publication of Pakistan International Airlines, August 1985.
19. *Price of Paradise,* Abdul Hye, P.O. Box-890071, Houston, TX 77289.

Qibla Direction

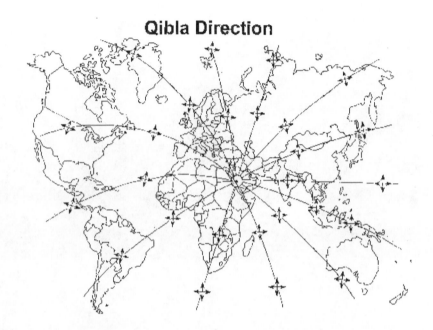